DK EYEWITNESS

KU-000-942

GREEK
PHRASE BOOK

Produced for DK by
Lexus Ltd with
Konstantinos Kontopidi-Greveniotis and
Antigoni Kamberou Miller

First published in Great Britain in 1997
by Dorling Kindersley Limited
80 Strand, London, WC2R 0RL

Reprinted with corrections 2000, 2003

A CIP catalogue record for this book is available from the British Library.
ISBN: 978-0-7513-2051-0

Printed in Latvia

A WORLD OF IDEAS:
SEE ALL THERE IS TO KNOW

www.dk.com

CONTENTS

ABOUT THIS BOOK

The *DK Eyewitness Greek Phrase Book* has been compiled by experts to meet the general needs of tourists and business travellers. Arranged under headings such as Hotels, Shopping, and so on, the ample selection of useful words and phrases is supported by a 1,800-line mini-dictionary. There is also an extensive menu guide listing approximately 600 dishes or methods of cooking and presentation.

Typical replies to questions you may ask during your journey, and the signs or instructions you may see or hear, are shown in tinted boxes. In the main text, the pronunciation of Greek words and phrases is imitated in English sound syllables. The Introduction gives basic guidelines to Greek pronunciation.

INTRODUCTION

Pronunciation

When reading the imitated pronunciation, stress the part that is underlined. Pronounce each syllable as if it formed part of an English word, and you will be understood sufficiently well. Remember the points below, and your pronunciation will be even closer to the correct Greek.

e   is always short, as in 'bed'

i   is always long, as in 'Lolita'

       (So when you see the imitation *ine*, remember to make this two syllables 'ee-ne'. Similarly, *ne* and *me* should be kept short – *don't* say 'nee' or 'mee'.)

g   should be a rolled, guttural sound at the back of the throat.

h   is a guttural 'ch', as in the Scottish 'loch'
       (*Don't* pronounce this as 'lock'.)

oo   long, as in 'moon'

th   as in 'then' or 'the'
       (Notice this particularly, and *don't* confuse it with TH in small capitals.)

TH   as in 'theatre' or 'thin'

Over the page is a further guide to Greek pronunciation, alongside the Greek alphabet (in both capital and lower-case letters).

THE GREEK ALPHABET

To help you read signs or notices printed in capital letters (which are sometimes quite unlike their lower-case counterparts), the Greek alphabet is given below. Alongside each letter is its name and a guide to its pronunciation. Until you get used to them, certain letters can be very confusing – for example, the **ro** which looks like an English 'P', or the lower-case **ni** which closely resembles an English 'v' (and is so similar to the small **ipsilon**).

letter		name	pronunciation
A	α	alfa	*a* as in 'father'
B	β	vita	*v* as in 'victory'
Γ	γ	ghamma	before *a*, *o* and *u* sounds, it is a guttural *gh* made at the back of the throat; before *e* and *i* sounds, it is like *y* in 'yes'
Δ	δ	dhelta	*th* as in 'then'
E	ε	epsilon	*e* as in 'end'
Z	ζ	zita	*z* as in 'zest'
H	η	ita	*i* as in 'Maria'
Θ	θ	thita	*th* as in 'theatre' (TH in the imitated pronunciation system)
I	ι	yiota	before *a* and *o* sounds, like *y* in 'yes'; otherwise like *i* in 'Maria'
K	κ	kapa	like *k* in 'king', but softer
Λ	λ	lamdha	*l* as in 'love'
M	μ	mi	*m* as in 'mother'
N	ν	ni	*n* as in 'no'

Ξ	ξ	ksi	*x* as in 'box', or *ks* as in 'books'
Ο	ο	omikron	*o* as in 'orange'
Π	π	pi	like *p* in 'Peter', but softer
Ρ	ρ	ro	*r* as in 'Rome', trilled or rolled
Σ	σ, ς	sighma	*s* as in 'sing'. The alternative small letter ς is used only at the end of a word
Τ	τ	taf	like *t* in 'tea', but softer
Υ	υ	ipsilon	*i* as in 'Maria'
Φ	φ	fi	*f* as in 'friend'
Χ	χ	hi	*ch* as in the Scottish 'loch'. But before *e* or *i* sounds, it is like *h* in 'hue'
Ψ	ψ	psi	like *ps* in 'lapse'
Ω	ω	omegha	*o* as in 'orange'

There are several letter combinations which result in totally different sounds. For example, the word for 'England' which you put on your postcards from Greece is Αγγλία (or ΑΓΓΛΙΑ in capitals), and one word for 'waiter' is γκαρσόνι or γκαρσόν: the combination γκ produces a hard 'g' as in 'go', while γγ makes an 'ng' as in 'England'.

Another combination that results in a new sound is ντ: most of the time this begins with a slight 'n' sound (like the 'nd' in 'bind'), but at the beginning of a word it is like the 'd' in 'dog' unless the previous word ends in a vowel. Don't worry about this – use either, but keep the 'n' ineffectual. Finally, the combination μπ is pronounced as in English 'b'.

Note that the Greek question mark is a semicolon. Stress is indicated by an accent above the Greek letter and an underline in the pronuciation.

USEFUL EVERYDAY PHRASES

Yes/No
Ναι/Όχι
ne/ohi

Thank you
Ευχαριστώ
efharisto

No, thank you
Όχι, ευχαριστώ
ohi efharisto

Please
Παρακαλώ
parakalo

I don't understand
Δεν καταλαβαίνω
then katalaveno

Do you speak English/French/German?
Μιλάτε Αγγλικά/Γαλλικά/Γερμανικά;
milate Anglika/Galika/Yermanika

I can't speak Greek
Δέν μιλάω Ελληνικά
then milao elinika

Please speak more slowly
Παρακαλώ, μιλάτε πιό αργά;
parakalo, milate pio arga

Please write it down for me
Μου το γράφετε, παρακαλώ;
moo to grafete, parakalo

Good morning/good afternoon/good night
Καλημέρα/καλησπέρα/καληνύχτα
kalimera/kalispera/kalinihta

Goodbye
Αντίο
andio

How are you?
Τι κάνεις;
ti kanis

Excuse me, please
Συγγνώμη, παρακαλώ
singnomi, parakalo

Sorry!
Συγγνώμη!
singnomi

I'm really sorry
Ειλικρινά, λυπάμαι
ilikrina, lipame

Can you help me?
Μπορείς να με βοηθήσεις;
boris na me voiTHisis

Can you tell me ...?
Μου λέτε ...;
moo lete

Can I have …?
Μπορώ να έχω …;
boro na eho

I would like …
Θα ήθελα …
THa iTHela

Is there … here?
Υπάρχει … εδώ;
iparhi … etho

Where are the toilets?
Που είναι οι τουαλέτες;
poo ine i tooaletes

Where can I get …?
Που μπορώ να πάρω …;
poo boro na paro

Is there wheelchair access?
Υπάρχει πρόσβαση για αναπηρικό καροτσάκι;
iparhi prosvasi ya anapiriko karotsaki

How much is it?
Πόσο κάνει;
poso kani

Do you take credit cards?
Δέχεστε πιστωτικές κάρτες;
theheste pistotikes kartes

Can I pay by cheque?
Μπορώ να πληρώσω με επιταγή;
boro na pliroso me epitayi

What time is it?
Τι ώρα είναι;
ti ora ine

I must go now
Πρέπει να πηγαίνω τώρα
prepi na piyeno tora

Cheers!
Εις υγείαν!
is iyian

Go away!
Παράτα με!
paratame

THINGS YOU'LL SEE OR HEAR

ανακοίνωση	*anakinosi*	announcement
ΑΝΑΧΩΡΗΣΕΙΣ/ αναχωρήσεις	*anahorisis*	departures
ΑΝΟΙΚΤΑ/ανοικτά	*anikta*	open
ΑΝΟΙΚΤΟΝ/ανοικτόν	*anikton*	open
ΑΣΑΝΣΕΡ/ασανσέρ	*asanser*	lift
αντίο	*andio*	goodbye
απαγορεύεται το κάπνισμα	*apagorevete to kapnisma*	no smoking
αργά	*arga*	slow
αριστερά	*aristera*	left
ΑΦΙΞΕΙΣ/αφίξεις	*afixis*	arrivals
βιβλιοθήκη	*vivliotHiki*	library
ΓΥΝΑΙΚΩΝ/γυναικών	*yinekon*	women
ΔΕΝ ΛΕΙΤΟΥΡΓΕΙ/ δεν λειτουργεί	*then litooryi*	out of order
δεξιά	*thexia*	right

→

11

διάλειμμα	thialima	interval
ΕΙΣΟΔΟΣ/είσοδος	isothos	way in, entrance
έκθεση	ekTHesi	exhibition, show room
έλεγχος	elenhos	check, inspection
ελεύθερος	elefTHeros	free
ΕΞΟΔΟΣ/έξοδος	exothos	way out
ευχαριστώ	efharisto	thank you
καλώς ήρθατε	kalos irTHate	welcome
ΚΑΠΝΙΖΟΝΤΕΣ/καπνίζοντες	kapnizodes	smokers
ΚΑΤΗΛΗΜΜΕΝΟΣ/ κατηλημμένος	katilimenos	engaged
ΚΙΝΔΥΝΟΣ/κίνδυνος	kinthinos	danger
ΚΛΕΙΣΤΑ/κλειστά	klista	closed
ΚΛΕΙΣΤΟΝ/κλειστόν	kliston	closed
μέχρι	mehri	until
μη	mi	do not
ναί	ne	yes
ορίστε;	oriste?	can I help you?
όχι	ohi	no
παρακαλώ	parakalo	please; can I help you?
πεζοί	pezi	pedestrians
προσοχή παρακαλώ	prosohi parakalo	attention, please
ΠΡΟΣΟΧΗ!/προσοχή!	prosohi	caution!
ΣΥΡΑΤΕ/σύρατε	sirate	pull
ΣΤΟΠ/στόπ	stop	stop
στρίψατε	stripsate	turn
ΣΧΟΛΕΙΟ/σχολείο	s-holio	school
ΤΑΜΕΙΟ/ταμείο	tamio	till, cash desk
ΤΕΛΩΝΕΙΟ/Τελωνείο	Telonio	Customs
ΤΟΥΡΙΣΤΙΚΗ ΑΣΤΥΝΟΜΙΑ/ Τουριστική Αστυνομία	Tooristiki Astinomia	Tourist Police
χαίρετε	herete	hello
ωθήσατε	oTHisate	push
ώρες λειτουργίας	ores litooryias	opening hours

DAYS, MONTHS, SEASONS

Sunday	Κυριακή	kiriaki
Monday	Δευτέρα	theftera
Tuesday	Τρίτη	triti
Wednesday	Τετάρτη	tetarti
Thursday	Πέμπτη	pembti
Friday	Παρασκευή	paraskevi
Saturday	Σάββατο	savato
January	Ιανουάριος	ianooarios
February	Φεβρουάριος	fevrooarios
March	Μάρτιος	martios
April	Απρίλιος	aprilios
May	Μάιος	maios
June	Ιούνιος	ioonios
July	Ιούλιος	ioolios
August	Αύγουστος	avgoostos
September	Σεπτέμβριος	septemvrios
October	Οκτώβριος	oktovrios
November	Νοέμβριος	noemvrios
December	Δεκέμβριος	thekemvrios
Spring	άνοιξη	anixi
Summer	καλοκαίρι	kalokeri
Autumn	φθινόπωρο	fтHinoporo
Winter	χειμώνας	himonas
Christmas	Χριστούγεννα	hristooyena
Christmas Eve	παραμονή Χριστουγέννων	paramoni hristooyenon
Good Friday	Μεγάλη Παρασκευή	megali paraskevi
Easter	Πάσχα	pas-ha
New Year	Πρωτοχρονιά	protohronia
New Year's Eve	Παραμονή Πρωτοχρονιάς	paramoni protohronias

NUMBERS

0 μηδέν *mithen*
1 ένα *ena*
2 δύο *thio*
3 τρία *tria*
4 τέσσερα *tesera*

5 πέντε *pende*
6 έξι *exi*
7 επτά *epta*
8 οχτώ *ohto*
9 εννιά *enia*

10 δέκα *theka*
11 έντεκα *edeka*
12 δώδεκα *thotheka*
13 δεκατρία *theka-tria*
14 δεκατέσσερα *theka-tesera*
15 δεκαπέντε *theka-pende*
16 δεκαέξι *theka-exi*
17 δεκαεπτά *theka-epta*
18 δεκαοκτώ *theka-ohto*
19 δεκαεννιά *theka-enia*
20 είκοσι *ikosi*
21 εικοσιένα *ikosi-ena*
22 εικοσιδύο *ikosi-thio*
30 τριάντα *trianda*
31 τριανταένα *trianda-ena*
32 τριανταδύο *trianda-thio*
40 σαράντα *saranda*
50 πενήντα *peninda*
60 εξήντα *exinda*
70 εβδομήντα *evthomida*
80 ογδόντα *ogthonda*
90 ενενήντα *eneninda*
100 εκατό *ekato*
110 εκατόν δέκα *ekaton theka*
200 διακόσια *thiakosia*
1,000 χίλια *hilia*
1,000,000 ένα εκατομμύριο *ena ekatomirio*

TIME

today	σήμερα	simera
yesterday	χτες	htes
tomorrow	αύριο	avrio
the day before yesterday	προχτές	prohtes
the day after tomorrow	μεθαύριο	meтнavrio
this week	αυτή την εβδομάδα	afti tin evthomatha
last week	την περασμένη εβδομάδα	tin perasmeni evthomatha
next week	την επόμενη εβδομάδα	tin epomeni evthomatha
this morning	το πρωί	to proi
this afternoon	το απόγευμα	to apoyevma
this evening	το βράδυ	to vrathi
tonight	απόψε	apopse
yesterday afternoon	χτες το απόγευμα	htes t'apoyevma
last night	χτες τη νύχτα	htes ti nihta
tomorrow morning	αύριο το πρωί	avrio to proi
tomorrow night	αύριο το βράδυ	avrio to vrathi
in three days	σε τρεις μέρες	se tris meres
three days ago	πριν τρεις μέρες	prin tris meres
late	αργά	arga
early	νωρίς	noris
soon	σύντομα	sindoma
later on	αργότερα	argotera
at the moment	προς το παρόν	pros to paron
second	το δευτερόλεπτο	to thefterolepto
minute	το λεπτό	to lepto
ten minutes	δέκα λεπτά	theka lepta
quarter of an hour	ένα τέταρτο	ena tetarto
half an hour	μισή ώρα	misi ora

three quarters of an hour	τρία τέταρτα της ώρας	tria tetarta tis oras
hour	ώρα	ora
day	μέρα	mera
week	εβδομάδα	evthomatha
fortnight	σε δύο εβδομάδες	se thio evthomathes
month	μήνας	minas
year	χρόνος	hronos

TELLING THE TIME

In Greek you always put the hour first and then use the word **ke** (και) to denote the minutes 'past' the hour and **para** (παρά) for the minutes 'to' the hour (eg 'five-twenty' = 5 **ke** 20; 'five-forty' = 6 **para** 20). The 24-hour clock is used officially in timetables and enquiry offices. Don't forget that Greek Standard Time is always two hours ahead of Greenwich Mean Time.

one o'clock	μία η ώρα	mia i ora
ten past one	μία και δέκα	mia ke theka
quarter past one	μία και τέταρτο	mia ke tetarto
twenty past one	μία και είκοσι	mia ke ikosi
half past one	μία και μισή	mia ke misi
twenty to two	δύο παρά είκοσι	thio para ikosi
quarter to two	δύο παρά τέταρτο	thio para tetarto
ten to two	δύο παρά δέκα	thio para theka
two o'clock	δύο η ώρα	thio i ora
13.00 (1 pm)	δεκατρείς	theka-tris
16.30 (4.30 pm)	δεκαέξι και τριάντα	theka-exi ke trianda
20.10 (8.10 pm)	είκοσι και δέκα	ikosi ke theka
at half past five	στις πέντε και μισή	stis pede ke misi
at seven o'clock	στις επτά	stis epta
noon	το μεσημέρι	to mesimeri
midnight	τα μεσάνυχτα	ta mesanihta

HOTELS

Depending on the visitor's preferences and on what they are prepared to spend, there is a choice of hotels, service flats, self-catering accommodation and rooms in private houses.

Hotels are divided into six categories: De Luxe or AA, and 1st to 5th Class or A to E. In most hotels a 15% service charge is added to your bill. The Greek National Tourist Organisation (EOT) publishes useful information with an up-to-date list of addresses and the facilities available. This may be obtained from their offices at 4 Conduit Street, London W1. If you are travelling in the high season it is always advisable to book accommodation in advance in the more popular areas.

USEFUL WORDS AND PHRASES

balcony	το μπαλκόνι	*to balkoni*
bathroom	το λουτρό	*to lootro*
bed	το κρεβάτι	*to krevati*
bedroom	το υπνοδωμάτιο	*to ipnothomatio*
bill	ο λογαριασμός	*o logariasmos*
breakfast	το πρωινό	*to proino*
dining room	η τραπεζαρία	*i trapezaria*
dinner	το δείπνο	*to thipno*
double room	το διπλό δωμάτιο	*to thiplo thomatio*
foyer	το φουαγέ	*to fooaye*
full board	η φουλ-πανσιόν	*i fool-pansion*
half board	η ντεμί-πανσιόν	*i demi-pansion*
hotel	το ξενοδοχείο	*to xenothohio*
key	το κλειδί	*to klithi*
lift	το ασανσέρ	*to asanser*
lounge	το σαλόνι	*to saloni*
lunch	το γεύμα	*to yevma*
manager	ο διευθυντής	*o thi-efthindis*
receipt	η απόδειξη	*i apothixi*
reception	η ρεσεψιόν	*i resepsion*

receptionist	ο ρεσεψιονίστας	o resepsionistas
restaurant	το εστιατόριο	to estiatorio
room	το δωμάτιο	to thomatio
room service	το σέρβις δωματίου	to servis thomatioo
shower	το ντους	to doos
single room	το μονό δωμάτιο	to mono thomatio
toilet	η τουαλέτα	i tooaleta
twin room	το δωμάτιο με δύο κρεβάτια	to thomatio me thio krevatia

Have you any vacancies?
Εχετε κενά δωμάτια;
ehete kena thomatia

I have a reservation
Εχω κλείσει δωμάτιο
eho klisi thomatio

I'd like a single room
Θα ήθελα ένα μονό δωμάτιο
THa ithela ena mono thomatio

I'd like a double room
Θα ήθελα ένα δωμάτιο με διπλό κρεβάτι
THa ithela ena thomatio me thiplo krevati

I'd like a twin room
Θα ήθελα ένα δωμάτιο με δύο κρεβάτια
THa ithela ena thomatio me thio krevatia

I'd like a room with a bathroom/balcony
Θα ήθελα ένα δωμάτιο με μπάνιο/μπαλκόνι
THa ithela ena thomatio me banio/balkoni

Is there satellite/cable TV in the rooms?
Τα δωμάτια έχουν δορυφοκή/καλωδιακή τηλεόραση;
ta thomatia ehoon thoriforiki/kalothiaki tileorasi

I'd like a room for one night/three nights
Θα ήθελα ένα δωμάτιο για μία νύχτα/τρεις νύχτες
THA itHela ena thomatio ya mia nihta/tris nihtes

What is the charge per night?
Πόσο στοιχίζει η διανυκτέρευση;
poso stihizi i thianihterefsi

I don't know yet how long I'll stay
Δεν ξέρω ακόμα πόσο καιρό θα μείνω
then xero akoma poso kero THA mino

When is breakfast/dinner?
Πότε έχει πρωινό/δείπνο;
pote ehi proino/thipno

Would you have my luggage brought up?
Θα μου φέρετε τις βαλίτσες μου;
THA moo ferete tis valitses moo

Please call me at ... o'clock
Παρακαλώ ειδοποιήστε με στις ...
parakalo ithopi-isteme stis ...

Can I have breakfast in my room?
Μπορώ να πάρω το πρωινό στο δωμάτιό μου;
boro na paro to proino sto thomatio moo

I'll be back at ... o'clock
Θα επιστρέψω στις ...
THA epistrepso stis ...

My room number is ...
Ο αριθμός του δωματιού μου είναι ...
o ariTHmos too thomatioo moo ine

I'm leaving tomorrow
Φεύγω αύριο
fevgo avrio

Can I have the bill, please?
Τον λογαριασμό παρακαλώ
ton logariasmo parakalo

Can you get me a taxi?
Μου καλείτε ένα ταξί;
moo kalite ena taxi

Can you recommend another hotel?
Μπορείτε να μου προτείνετε κάποιο άλλο ξενοδοχείο;
borite na moo protinete kapio alo xenothohio

THINGS YOU'LL HEAR

Then iparhoon mona/thipla thomatia kena
There are no single/double rooms left

Imaste yemati
No vacancies

Parakalo, plironete prokatavolika
Please pay in advance

Parakalo, afinete to thiavatsrio sas etho
Please leave your passport here

THINGS YOU'LL SEE

ασανσέρ	asanser	lift, elevator
γκαράζ	garaz	garage
δείπνο	thipno	dinner
διπλό δωμάτιο	thiplo thomatio	double room
δωμάτια	thomatia	rooms
είσοδος	isothos	entrance
ενοικιάζονται δωμάτια	enikianzode thomatia	rooms to let
ΕΟΤ		Greek National Tourist Organisation
έξοδος κινδύνου	exothos kinthinoo	emergency exit
εστιατόριο	estiatorio	restaurant
ισόγειο	isoyio	ground floor
λογαριασμός	logariasmos	bill
λουτρό	lootro	bathroom
μονό δωμάτιο	mono thomatio	single room
ντους	doos	shower
ξενοδοχείο	xenothohio	hotel
πλήρες	plires	full, no vacancies
πρωινό	proino	breakfast
πρώτος όροφος	protos orofos	first floor
ρεσεψιόν	resepsion	reception
σκάλες	skales	stairs
σύρατε	sirate	pull
τουαλέτες	tooaletes	toilets
υπόγειο	ipoyio	basement
φαγητό	fayito	meal, lunch
ωθήσατε	oThisate	push

CAMPING AND CARAVANNING

There are plenty of organised camping sites run by EOT
(the Greek National Tourist Organisation), and often these are
situated in some of the most picturesque parts of the country.
Campsites are usually open from March to November. In
addition to the state-run campsites there are also a large number
of sites run by private individuals under licence. Further details
about these camping sites can be supplied by EOT information
offices in Greece or in London, as well as by the Greek Tourist
Police, who have an office in every major Greek town. If you
are camping in Greece you should remember that it is
forbidden to camp anywhere other than in a proper site.

Youth hostels are open to members of the YHA (Youth Hostels
Association). Stays are limited to ten nights.

USEFUL WORDS AND PHRASES

bucket	ο κουβάς	o koovas
campfire	φωτιά	fotia
go camping	κατασκηνώνω	kataskinono
campsite	το κάμπινγκ	to 'camping'
caravan	το τροχόσπιτο	to trohospito
caravan site	το κάμπινγκ για τροχόσπιτα	to 'camping' ya trohospita
cooking utensils	τα σκεύη μαγειρικής	ta skevi mayirikis
drinking water	το πόσιμο νερό	to posimo nero
groundsheet	ο μουσαμάς	o moosamas
hitchhike	κάνω ωτο-στόπ	kano oto-stop
rope	το σχοινί	to s-hini
rubbish	τα σκουπίδια	ta skoopithia
rucksack	το σακίδιο	to sakithio
saucepans	τα κατσαρολικά	ta katsarolika
sleeping bag	το σλίπινγκ μπαγκ	to 'sleeping bag'
tent	η σκηνή	i skini
youth hostel	ο ξενώνας νέων	o xenonas neon

Can I camp here?
Μπορώ να κατασκηνώσω εδώ;
boro na kataskinoso etho

Can we park the caravan here?
Μπορούμε να παρκάρουμε το τροχόσπιτο εδώ;
boroome na parkaroome to trohospito etho

Where is the nearest campsite?
Που είναι το πλησιέστερο κάμπινγκ;
poo ine to plisi-estero 'camping'

What is the charge per night?
Πόσο στοιχίζει η διανυκτέρευση;
poso stihizi i thianikterefsi

What facilities are there?
Τι ευκολίες υπάρχουν εκεί;
ti efkoli-es iparhoon eki

Can I light a fire here?
Μπορώ ν' ανάψω φωτιά εδώ;
boro n' anapso fotia etho

Where can I get ...?
Που μπορώ να βρώ ...;
poo boro na vro

Is there drinking water here?
Υπάρχει πόσιμο νερό εδώ;
iparhi posimo nero etho

THINGS YOU'LL SEE

απαγορεύεται	*apagorevete*	no camping
το κάμπινγκ	*to 'camping'*	
κάμπινγκ	*'camping'*	campsite
κουβέρτα	*kooverta*	blanket
κουζίνα	*koozina*	kitchen
νερό	*nero*	water
ντους	*doos*	shower
ξενώνας νέων	*xenonas neon*	youth hostel
πόσιμο νερό	*posimo nero*	drinking water
ριμουλκό	*rimoolko*	trailer
		(camping etc)
σκηνή	*skini*	tent
σλίπινγκ μπαγκ	*'sleeping bag'*	sleeping bag
ταυτότητα	*taftotita*	pass,
		identity card
τιμή	*timi*	charges
τουαλέτες	*tooaletes*	toilets
τροχόσπιτα	*trohospita*	caravans
φως	*fos*	light
φωτιά	*fotia*	fire
χρησιμοποιείται ...	*hrisimopi-ite*	use ...

DRIVING

Most roads in Greece are single-lane only. The national highways (*eTHniki*) are the best to use, as they often have crawler lanes for heavy vehicles, which makes overtaking much easier. They join Patra with Athens if you are coming by ferry from Italy, and the Greek-Macedonian border with Thessaloniki and Athens if you are coming into Greece through Austria and the former Yugoslavia. Secondary roads are not so good and can often be in quite poor condition. Holders of British driving licences do not need an international driving licence.

The Greek Automobile and Touring Club (ELPA) offers assistance to foreign motorists free of charge if they are members of the AA or RAC. However, you may be better off arranging European cover with the AA or RAC before you travel. When hiring a car or a motorbike you might find that your passport will be kept until you return.

The rules of the road are: drive on the right, overtake on the left. Priority at crossroads is as indicated by standard international signs. At crossroads without road signs, vehicles coming from the right have priority. Seat belts are compulsory. Children under 10 years old must not travel in the front seat.

The speed limit on the national highways is 120 km/h (75 mph) for cars, 90 km/h (55 mph) for motorbikes over 100cc and 70 km/h (45 mph) for motorbikes under 100cc, otherwise keep to the speed shown. In built-up areas the limit is 50 km/h (31 mph).

There are plenty of service stations around the main towns but they can be few and far between in the countryside. Fuel ratings are as follows: super (4-star), unleaded and diesel. Petrol stations on the highways are usually open 24 hours a day but elsewhere they close early at night.

SOME COMMON ROAD SIGNS

αδιέξοδο	*athiexotho*	cul-de-sac, dead end
απαγορεύεται η στάθμευση	*apagorevete i staTHmefsi*	no parking
γραμμές τραίνου	*grames trenoo*	railway crosses road
διάβαση πεζών	*thiavasi pezon*	pedestrian crossing
διόδια	*thiothia*	toll
έξοδος αυτοκινήτων	*exothos aftokiniton*	vehicle exit
έργα	*erga*	roadworks
ιδιωτικός δρόμος	*ithiotikos thromos*	private road
ισόπεδος διάβασις	*isopethos thiavasis*	level crossing, railway crossing
κάμπινγκ	*'camping'*	campsite
κέντρο	*kendro*	centre
κίνδυνος πυρκαγιάς	*kinthinos pirkayas*	fire risk
μονόδρομος	*monothromos*	one-way street
νομός	*nomos*	county
οδός	*othos*	street, road
παραλία	*paralia*	beach
πεζοί	*pezi*	pedestrians
πρατήριο βενζίνης	*pratirio venzinis*	petrol station
προσοχή	*prosohi*	caution
στοπ	*'stop'*	stop
σχολείο	*s-holio*	school
τέλος	*telos*	end
τροχαία	*trohea*	traffic police
χιλιόμετρα	*hiliometra*	kilometres

USEFUL WORDS AND PHRASES

bonnet	το καπό	to kapo
boot	το πορτ-μπαγκάζ	to port-bagaz
brake	το φρένο	to freno
breakdown	η μηχανική βλάβη	i mihaniki vlavi
car	το αυτοκίνητο	to aftokinito
caravan	το τροχόσπιτο	to trohospito
car seat	η παιδική καρέκλα αυτοκινήτου	i pethiki karekla aftokinitou
(for a baby)		
crossroads	η διασταύρωση	i thiastavrosi
to drive	οδηγώ	othigo
engine	η μηχανή	i mihani
exhaust	η εξάτμηση	i exatmisi
fanbelt	το λουρί του βεντιλατέρ	to loori too ventilater
garage (for repairs)	το συνεργείο	to sineryio
(for petrol)	το βενζινάδικο	to venzinathiko
gear	η ταχύτητα	i tahitita
gears	οι ταχύτητες	i tahitites
junction (motorway)	η έξοδος	i exothos
licence	το δίπλωμα οδηγού	to thiploma othiyoo
lights (head)	τα μπροστινά φώτα	ta brostina fota
(rear)	τα πίσω φώτα	ta piso fota
lorry	το φορτηγό	to fortigo
mirror	ο καθρέφτης	o kaTHreftis
motorbike	το μηχανάκι	to mihanaki
motorway	η εθνική οδός	i eTHniki othos
number plate	οι πινακίδες	i pinakithes
petrol	η βενζίνη	i venzini
road	ο δρόμος	o thromos
skid (verb)	γλυστράω	glistrao
spares	τα ανταλακτικά	ta andalaktika

speed	η ταχύτητα	i tahitita
speed limit	το όριο ταχύτητας	to orio tahititas
speedometer	το κοντέρ	to konter
steering wheel	το τιμόνι	to timoni
tow (*verb*)	τραβάω	travao
traffic lights	τα φανάρια	ta fanaria
trailer	το ριμουλκό	to rimoolko
tyre	το λάστιχο	to lastiho
van	το φορτηγάκι	to fortigaki
wheel	η ρόδα	i rotha
windscreen	το παρμπρίζ	to parbriz

I'd like some petrol
Θέλω βενζίνη
THelo venzini

I'd like some oil/water
Θέλω λάδι/νερό
THelo lathi/nero

Fill it up, please
Το γεμίζετε παρακαλώ;
to yemizete, parakalo

I'd like 10 litres of petrol
Θέλω δέκα λίτρα βενζίνη
THelo theka litra venzini

How do I get to …?
Πως μπορώ να πάω …;
pos boro na pao

Is this the road to …?
Αυτός είναι ο δρόμος για …;
aftos ine o thromos ya

DIRECTIONS YOU MAY BE GIVEN

efthia	straight on
pernas to/ti ...	go past the ...
st'aristera	on the left
sta thexia	on the right
stripse aristera	turn left
stripse thexia	turn right
theftero aristera	second on the left
to proto thexia	first on the right

Where is the nearest garage?
Πού είναι το πλησιέστερο βενζινάδικο;
poo ine to plisi-estero venzinathiko

Would you check the tyres, please?
Ελέγχετε τα λάστιχα, παρακαλώ;
elenhete ta lastiha, parakalo

Do you do repairs?
Κάνετε επισκευές;
kanete episkeves

Can you repair the clutch?
Μου φτιάχνετε το ντεμπραγιάζ;
moo ftiahnete to debrayaz

How long will it take?
Πόσο θα κάνει;
poso tha kani

There is something wrong with the engine
Κάτι δεν πάει καλά με τη μηχανή
kati then pai kala me ti mihani

The engine is overheating
Η μηχανή υπερθερμαίνεται
i mihani iperτHermenete

The brakes are binding
Τα φρένα κολλάνε
ta frena kolane

I need a new tyre
Χρειάζομαι καινούργιο λάστιχο
hriazome kenooryio lastiho

Where can I park?
Που μπορώ να παρκάρω;
poo boro na parkaro

Can I park here?
Μπορώ να παρκάρω εδώ;
boro na parkaro etho

I'd like to hire a car
Θέλω να νοικιάσω ένα αυτοκίνητο
τHelo na nikiaso ena aftokinito

THINGS YOU'LL SEE

αεραντλία	*aerandlia*	air pump
αλλαγή λαδιών	*alayi lathion*	oil change
ανοικτόν	*anikton*	open
ανταλλακτικά αυτοκινήτων	*andalaktika aftokiniton*	car spares
αντιπροσωπεία αυτοκινήτων	*andiprosopia aftokiniton*	car dealer
αντλία βενζίνης	*andlia venzinis*	petrol pump
απλή	*apli*	regular

→

αστυνομία	astinomia	police
βαφές αυτοκινήτων	vafes aftokiniton	car body shop
βενζίνη	venzini	petrol
βουλκανιζατέρ	voolkanizater	tyre repairs
γκαράζ	garaz	garage (for parking)
εθνική οδός	eTHniki othos	motorway
ελαστικά	elastika	tyres
ενοικιάζονται αυτοκίνητα	enikiazonde aftokinita	car rental
εξατμίσεις	exatmisis	exhausts
έξοδος	exothos	exit, way out
ηλεκτρολόγος αυτοκινήτων	ilektrologos aftokiniton	car electrician
λάδια	lathia	engine oil
σβήστε τη μηχανή	sviste ti mihani	switch off engine
σούπερ	'super'	4-star petrol
συνεργείο	sineryio	car repairs

RAIL AND BOAT TRAVEL

Hellenic Railways Organization (ΟΣΕ) operates the country's railway network. The trains are modern, and there are regular and comfortable services to the most important regions of the mainland. Otherwise, the network is not very extensive. In the summer, it is worth booking tickets in advance as the trains can get very busy. There are first and second class season tickets at reduced rates which permit the holder to travel as many times as they wish. Trains are cheap, a return ticket costing 20% less than two singles. Children 14 or under travel at half price.

Boats connect the mainland with all the major islands, and there are frequent ferries to most islands from Piraeus. Greece also has a many catamaran and hydrofoil services. These are faster than ferries but are more expensive. You should book your tickets in advance for all boat services. Altogether there are some 200 ports in the Greek islands and 50 ports on the mainland. The islands are interconnected by sea routes and, for excursions, there are daily around-the-island trips or visits to other nearby islands.

Useful Words and Phrases

boat	το πλο›ο	to plio
booking office	το πρακτορε›ο	to praktorio
buffet	το μπαρ	to bar
car ferry	το φέρρυ-μπωτ	to feri-bot
carriage	το βαγόνι	to vagoni
connection	η σ‡νδεση	i sinthesi
currency exchange	το συνάλλαγμα	to sinalagma
dining car	η τραπεζαρ›α του τρανου	i trapezaria too trenoo
engine	η μηχαν‹	i mihani
entrance	η ε›σοδος	i isothos

32

exit	η έξοδος	i exothos
ferry	το φέρρυ-μπωτ	to feri-bot
first class	η πρώτη θέση	i proti THesi
get in	μπαίνω	beno
get out	βγαίνω	v-yeno
left luggage	ο χώρος φύλαξης αποσκευών	o horos filaxis aposkevon
lost property	τα απολεσθέντα αντικείμενα	ta apoles-THenda andikimena
luggage trolley	το καροτσάκι	to karotsaki
platform	η πλατφόρμα	i platforma
port	το λιμάνι	to limani
quay	η προκυμαία	i prokimea
rail	οι γραμμές	i grames
railway	ο σιδηρόδρομος	o sithirothromos
reserved seat	η κλεισμένη θέση	i klismeni THesi
restaurant car	το βαγόνι εστιατόριου	to vagoni estiatorioo
return ticket	το εισιτήριο μετ'επιστροφής	to isitirio metepistrofis
sea	η θάλασσα	i THalasa
seat	η θέση	i THesi
ship	το πλοίο	to plio
station	ο σταθμός	o staTHmos
station master	ο σταθμάρχης	o staTHmarhis
ticket	το εισιτήριο	to isitirio
ticket collector	ο εισπράκτορας	o ispraktoras
timetable	τα δρομολόγια	ta thromoloyia
train	το τραίνο	to treno
waiting room	η αίθουσα αναμονής	i eTHoosa anamonis
window	το παράθυρο	to paraTHiro

When does the boat for … leave?
Πότε φεύγει το πλοίο για …;
pote fev-yi to plio ya

When does the train from … arrive?
Πότε έρχεται το τραίνο από …;
pote erhete to treno apo

When is the next/first/last boat to …?
Πότε είναι το επόμενο/πρώτο/τελευταίο πλοίο για …;
pote ine to epomeno/proto/telefteo plio ya

What is the fare to …?
Πόσο κάνει το εισιτήριο για …;
poso kani to isitirio ya

Is there a reduction for children?
Υπάρχει μειωμένο εισιτήριο για παιδιά;
iparhi miomeno isitirio ya pethia

Do I have to change?
Πρέπει ν'αλλάξω;
prepi nalaxo

Does the boat/train stop at …?
Σταματάει στη …;
stamatai sti

How long does it take to get to …?
Πόσες ώρες κάνει να φθάσει …;
poses ores kani na ftHasi

A single/return ticket to …, please
Ένα απλό/μετ'επιστροφής εισιτήριο για … παρακαλώ
ena aplo/metepistrofis isitirio ya … parakalo

I'd like to reserve a seat
Θέλω να κλείσω μία θέση
tHelo na kliso mia tHesi

Is this the right boat for ...?
Αυτό είναι το πλοίο για ...;
afto ine to plio ya

Is there a car ferry to ...?
Υπάρχει φέρρυ-μπωτ για ...;
iparhi feri-bot ya

Is this the right platform for the ... train?
Αυτή είναι η σωστή πλατφόρμα γιά το τραίνο προς ...;
afti ine i sosti platforma ya to treno pros

Which platform for the ... train?
Σε ποιά πλατφόρμα γιά το τραίνο προς ...;
se pia platforma ya to treno pros

Is the boat late?
Έχει καθυστέρηση το πλοίο;
ehi kaτhisterisi to plio

Could you help me with my luggage, please?
Μπορείτε να με βοηθήσετε με τις αποσκευές μου, παρακαλώ;
borite na me voiτhisete me tis aposkeves moo, parakalo

Is this a non-smoking compartment?
Είναι για τους μη καπνίζοντες;
ine ya toos mi kapnizondes

Is this seat free?
Είναι ελεύθερη αυτή η θέση;
ine elefτheri afti i τhesi

This seat is taken
Αυτή η θέση είναι πιασμένη
afti i τhesi ine piasmeni

I have reserved this seat
Έχω κλείσει αυτή τη θέση
eho klisi afti ti THesi

May I open/close the window?
Μπορώ ν'ανοίξω/κλείσω το παράθυρο;
boro nanixo/kliso to paraTHiro

When do we arrive in ...?
Πότε φτάνουμε στη ...;
pote ftanoome sti

Which island is this?
Ποιό νησί είναι αυτό;
pio nisi ine afto

Do we stop at ...?
Σταματάμε στη ...;
stamatame sti

Is there a restaurant car on this train?
Υπάρχει βαγόνι εστιατορίου σ'αυτό το τραίνο;
iparhi vagoni estiatorioo safto to treno

THINGS YOU'LL SEE

ακριβές αντίτιμο μόνο	*akrives anditimo mono*	exact fare only
ακτή	*akti*	beach
αριθμός θέσεως	*ariTHmos THeseos*	seat number
αφετηρία	*afetiria*	terminus
διαβατήρια	*thiavatiria*	passports
δρομολόγια	*thromologia*	timetable
εισιτήρια	*isitiria*	tickets
καμπίνες	*kabines*	cabins

➡

καπετάνιος	*kapetanios*	captain
κατάστρωμα	*katastroma*	deck
λέμβος	*lemvos*	lifeboat
λιμενάρχης	*limenarhis*	harbour master
λιμήν	*limin*	port, harbour
λογιστήριο	*loyistirio*	purser's office
Ο/Γ		ferry
ΟΣΕ	*ose*	Hellenic Railways Organization
προς γκαράζ	*pros garaz*	to car deck
σωσίβια	*sosivia*	life jackets
τουαλέτες	*tooaletes*	toilets
τραπεζαρία	*trapezaria*	dining room (boat)

Questions You May Be Asked

Ti aftokinito ine?
What type of car is it?

Ti mikos ehi to aftokinito?
What is the length of your car?

AIR TRAVEL

Air services connect Greece with all the major airports of the world. Olympic Airlines and many other international and British airlines provide services between major cities in the UK and the following Greek destinations: Athens, Thessaloniki, and the islands of Corfu, Rhodes, Crete and Mikonos. There is also an extensive domestic network run by Olympic Airways (OA) connecting the main towns, islands and tourist centres. In Athens the eastern terminal serves all foreign airlines, and the western terminal caters for all domestic and international OA flights.

USEFUL WORDS AND PHRASES

air bus	το λεωφορείο του αεροδρομίου	to leoforio too aerothromioo
aircraft	το αεροπλάνο	to aeroplano
air hostess	η αεροσυνοδός	i aerosinothos
airline	οι αερογραμμές	i aerogrames
airport	το αεροδρόμιο	to aerothromio
aisle seat	η θέση δίπλα στο διάδρομο	i THesi thipla sto thiathromo
baggage claim	οι αποσκευές	i aposkeves
boarding card	η κάρτα αναχώρησης	i karta anahorisis
check-in	το τσεκ-ιν	to 'check-in'
delay	η καθυστέρηση	i kaTHisterisi
departure	η αναχώρηση	i anahorisi
departure lounge	η αίθουσα αναχωρήσεων	i eTHoosa anahoriseon
emergency exit	η έξοδος κινδύνου	i exothos kinthinoo
flight	η πτήση	i ptisi
flight number	ο αριθμός πτήσεως	o ariTHmos ptiseos
gate	η έξοδος	i exothos
jet	το τζετ	to 'jet'

land	προσγειώνομαι	*prosyionome*
passport	το διαβατήριο	*to thiavatirio*
passport control	ο έλεγχος διαβατηρίων	*o elenhos thiavatirion*
pilot	ο πιλότος	*o pilotos*
runway	ο διάδρομος	*o thiathromos*
seat	η θέση	*i THesi*
seat belt	η ζώνη ασφαλείας	*i zoni asfalias*
steward	ο αεροσυνοδός	*o aerosinothos*
take off	απογειώνομαι	*apoyionome*
window	το παράθυρο	*to paraTHiro*
wing	το φτερό	*to ftero*

When is there a flight to …?
Πότε έχει πτήση για …;
pote ehi ptisi ya

What time does the flight to … leave?
Τί ώρα φεύγει η πτήση για …;
ti ora fevyi i ptisi ya

Is it a direct flight?
Υπάρχει κατευθείαν πτήση;
iparhi katefTHian ptisi

Do I have to change planes?
Πρέπει ν'αλλάξω αεροπλάνο;
prepi nalaxo aeroplano

When do I have to check in?
Πότε πρέπει να δώσω τις αποσκευές μου;
pote prepi na thoso tis aposkeves moo

I'd like a single/return ticket to …
Θα ήθελα ένα απλό/μετ'επιστροφής εισιτήριο γιά …
THA iTHela ena aplo/metepistrofis isitirio ya

I'd like a non-smoking seat, please
Θέλω μία θέση στους μη καπνίζοντες, παρακαλώ
THelo mia THesi stoos mi kapnizondes, parakalo

I'd like a window seat, please
Θέλω μία θέση με παράθυρο, παρακαλώ
THelo mia THesi me paraTHiro, parakalo

How long will the flight be delayed?
Ποσο θα καθυστερήσει η πτήση;
poso THa katHisterisi i ptisi

Is this the right gate for the ... flight?
Αυτή είναι η σωστή έξοδος γιά την πτήση ...;
afti ine i sosti exothos ya tin ptisi

When do we arrive in ...?
Πότε φτάνουμε ...;
pote ftanoome

May I smoke now?
Επιτρέπετε να καπνίσω τώρα;
epitrepete na kapniso tora

I do not feel very well
Δεν αισθάνομαι καλά
THen estHanome kala

THINGS YOU'LL SEE OR HEAR

ΟΑ	*Olimbiakí*	Olympic Airways
αεροδρόμιο	*aerothrómio*	airport
αερολιμήν	*aerolimín*	airport
αεροσυνοδός	*aerosinothós*	air hostess
αναχωρίσεις	*anahorísis*	departures
απαγορεύεται το κάπνισμα	*apagorevete to kapnisma*	no smoking
αφίξεις	*afíxis*	arrivals
διάδρομος	*thiáthromos*	runway
διάρκεια πτήσεως	*thiárkia ptíseos*	flight time
δρομολόγια	*thromolóyia*	timetable
έλεγχος διαβατηρίων	*élenhos thiavatiríon*	passport control
έξοδος	*éxothos*	exit, gate, door
έξοδος κινδύνου	*éxothos kinthínoo*	emergency exit
επιβάτες	*epivátes*	passengers
κυβερνήτης	*kivernítis*	captain
πληροφορίες	*pliroforíes*	information
πλήρωμα	*plíroma*	crew
προσδεθήτε	*pros-theTHíte*	fasten your seat belt
πτήσεις εξωτερικού	*ptísis exoterikoo*	international flights
πτήσεις εσωτερικού	*ptísis esoterikoo*	domestic flights
τοπική ώρα	*topikí óra*	local time
ύψος	*ípsos*	altitude

BUS, TAXI AND UNDERGROUND TRAVEL

Greek cities all have good bus networks. In Athens there are
electric trolleys in addition to the bus services. You buy your
ticket before boarding the bus or trolley. It must then be
stamped in a special ticket machine when you board. There is
a penalty fine for not stamping your ticket.

The main towns are connected by an excellent network of
long-distance buses, which run punctually and more than
make up for the less than extensive railway network. The
buses are comfortable, fast and often have air conditioning.
Tickets are bought at the terminal before boarding for the
long-distance services.

Taxis are plentiful in Greece, cheaper than in western Europe
and used much more frequently. They are yellow or sometimes
grey and are marked ΤΑΞΙ. For short local journeys you pay by
the kilometre, and the fare is displayed on the meter. For longer
drives, ask the fare in advance.

Only Athens has an underground system, which is called
Ο ΗΛΕΚΤΡΙΚΟΣ (o ilektrikos) and which joins Piraeus with
Athens and Kifisia.

USEFUL WORDS AND PHRASES

bus	το λεωφορείο	to leoforio
bus stop	η στάση	i stasi
child	το παιδί	to pethi
coach	το πούλμαν	to poolman
conductor	ο εισπράκτορας	o ispraktoras
connection	η σύνδεση	i sinthesi
driver	ο οδηγός	o othigos
fare	η τιμή	i timi
lake	η λίμνη	i limni
number 5 bus	το πέντε	to pende
passenger	ο επιβάτης	o epivatis
port	το λιμάνι	to limani

river	το ποτάμι	*to potami*
sea	η θάλασσα	*i THalasa*
seat	η θέση	*i THesi*
station	ο σταθμός	*o staTHmos*
taxi	το ταξί	*to taxi*
ticket	το εισιτήριο	*to isitirio*
underground	ο ηλεκτρικός	*o ilektrikos*

Where is the nearest underground station?
Που είναι ο πλησιέστερος σταθμός του ηλεκτρικού;
poo ine o plisi-esteros staTHmos too ilektrikoo

Where is the bus station?
Που είναι ο σταθμός των υπεραστικών λεωφορίων;
poo ine o staTHmos ton iperastikon leoforion

Where is the bus stop?
Που είναι η στάση;
poo ine i stasi

Which buses go to …?
Ποιά λεωφορεία πάνε στο …;
pia leoforia pane sto

How often do the buses to … run?
Πόσο συχνά έχει λεωφορείο γιά …;
poso sihna ehi leoforio ya

Would you tell me when we get to …?
Μπορείτε να μου πείτε πότε φτάνουμε στο …;
borite na moo pite pote ftanoome sto

Do I get off here?
Πρέπει να κατέβω εδώ;
prepi na katevo etho

How do you get to …?
Πως πάμε στο …;
pos pame sto

Is it very far?
Είναι πολύ μακριά;
ine poli makria

I want to go to …
Θέλω να πάω στο …
THelo na pao sto

Do you go near …?
Πάτε κοντά στο …;
pate konda sto

Where can I buy a ticket?
Από πού μπορώ ν'αγοράσω ένα εισιτήριο;
apo poo boro nagoraso ena isitirio

Please open/close the window
Παρακαλώ, ανοίγετε/κλείνετε το παράθυρο;
parakalo, aniyete/klinete to paraTHiro

Could you help me get a ticket?
Μπορείτε να με βοηθήσετε να βγάλω ένα εισιτήριο;
borite na me voiTHisete na vgalo ena isitirio

When does the last bus leave?
Πότε φεύγει το τελευταίο λεωφορείο;
pote fevyi to telefteo leofirio

THINGS YOU'LL SEE

Απαγορεύεται	apagorevete	no entry
η είσοδος	i isothos	
γραμμή	grami	route
εισιτήρια	isitiria	tickets
έλεγχος εισιτηρίων	elenhos isitirion	ticket inspection
ελεύθερον	elefтHeron	for hire (taxis)
ηλεκτρικός	ilektrikos	underground
θέσεις	тHesis	seats
μην ομιλείτε	min omilite	do not speak to
στον οδηγό	ston othigo	the driver
οδηγός	othigos	driver
ορθίων	orтHion	standing
παιδικό	pethiko	children
πρόστιμο	prostimo	fine (penalty)
πυροσβεστήρ	pirosvestir	fire extinguisher
σταθμός ταξί	staтHmos taxi	taxi stand
σταθμός	staтHmos	bus station
υπεραστικών	iperastikon	(long-distance)
λεωφορείων	leoforion	
στάσις	stasis	bus stop
ταξί	taxi	taxi
ταρίφα	tarifa	taxi tariff
χωρητικότητος	horitikotitos	maximum load
... ατόμων	... atomon	... persons
χωρις εισπράκτορα	horis ispraktora	no ticket collector

EATING OUT

Some examples of places to eat and drink are shown below
(notice that signs in Greek capital letters often look different
from the same words in lower-case).

ΕΣΤΙΑΤΟΡΙΟΝ Εστιατόριον *estiatorion* (restaurant)
In all tourist places you will find the menu printed in English
as well as in Greek, and the staff will almost certainly speak
English. If you feel more adventurous, you might prefer to try
some of the many Greek delicacies available, and in smaller
places you will be welcomed into the kitchen to see what's
cooking. In Greek restaurants you are provided with water and
bread without ordering. The menu will usually give you two
prices for each item – the higher one includes a service charge.

ΤΑΒΕΡΝΑ Ταβέρνα *taverna*
This is a typical Greek restaurant, where draught wine is
available. (Note that wine is ordered by weight not by volume,
so you might order a kilo, not a litre.)

ΨΑΡΟΤΑΒΕΡΝΑ Ψαροταβέρνα *psarotaverna*
A restaurant specializing in seafood.

ΨΗΣΤΑΡΙΑ Ψησταριά *psistaria*
A restaurant specializing in charcoal-grilled food.

ΟΥΖΕΡΙ Ουζερί *oozeri*
A bar that serves ouzo (a strong, aniseed-flavoured spirit) and
beer with snacks (called **mezethes**) served as side-dishes –
these snacks could be savouries or sometimes, and especially
in the islands, octopus or local seafood.

ΖΑΧΑΡΟΠΛΑΣΤΕΙΟ Ζαχαροπλαστείο *zaharoplastio*
A pastry shop or café that serves cakes and soft drinks and is
also an ideal place to have breakfast.

ΚΑΦΕΝΕΙΟ Καφενείο *kafenio*
A coffee house, where Greek coffee is served with traditional
sweets. Here you can play a game of cards or backgammon.
Greek women are rarely seen here.

USEFUL WORDS AND PHRASES

beer	η μπύρα	*i bira*
bill	ο λογαριασμός	*o logariasmos*
bottle	το μπουκάλι	*to bookali*
cake	το γλυκό	*to gliko*
chef	ο μάγειρας	*o mayiras*
coffee	ο καφές	*o kafes*
cup	το φλυτζάνι	*to flitzani*
fork	το πιρούνι	*to pirooni*
glass	το ποτήρι	*to potiri*
knife	το μαχαίρι	*to maheri*
menu	το μενού	*to menoo*
milk	το γάλα	*to gala*
napkin	η χαρτοπετσέτα	*i hartopetseta*
plate	το πιάτο	*to piato*
receipt	η απόδειξη	*i apothixi*
sandwich	το σάντουιτς	*to sandooits*
soup	η σούπα	*i soopa*
spoon	το κουτάλι	*to kootali*
sugar	η ζάχαρη	*i zahari*
table	το τραπέζι	*to trapezi*
tea	το τσάι	*to tsai*
teaspoon	το κουταλάκι	*to kootalaki*
tip	το πουρμπουάρ	*to poorbooar*
waiter	ο σερβιτόρος	*o servitoros*
waitress	η σερβιτόρα	*i servitora*
water	το νερό	*to nero*
wine	το κρασί	*to krasi*
wine list	ο κατάλογος	*o katalogos*
	κρασιών	*krasion*

A table for 1/2/3, please
Ένα τραπέζι για ένα/δύο/τρία άτομα, παρακαλώ
ena trapezi ya ena/thio/tria atoma, parakalo

Can we see the menu?
Μπορούμε να δούμε το μενού;
boroome na thoome to menoo

Can we see the wine list?
Μπορούμε να δούμε τον κατάλογο των κρασιών;
boroome na thoome ton katalogo ton krasion

Is there a highchair?
Υπάρχει παιδική καρέκλα;
iparhi pethiki karekla

What would you recommend?
Τι θα προτείνατε;
ti тна protinate

Is this suitable for vegetarians?
Είναι για χορτοφάγους;
Ine ya hortofagoos

I'd like ...
Θα ήθελα ...
тна iтнela

Just a cup of coffee, please
Μόνο ένα φλυτζάνι καφέ, παρακαλώ
mono ena flitzani kafe, parakalo

A kilo/half a kilo of retsina
Ένα κιλό/μισό κιλό ρετσίνα
ena kilo/miso kilo retsina

Waiter!
Γκαρσόν!
garson

Can we have the bill, please?
Μας φέρνετε τον λογαριασμό, παρακαλώ;
mas fernete ton logariasmo, parakalo

I only want a snack
Θέλω κάτι ελαφρύ
THelo kati elafri

I didn't order this
Δεν παράγγειλα αυτό
then parangila afto

May we have some more ...?
Μπορούμε να έχουμε ακόμη λίγο ...;
boroome na ehoome akomi ligo

The meal was very good, thank you
Το φαγητό ήταν πολύ καλό, ευχαριστούμε
to fayito itan poli kalo, efharistoome

My compliments to the chef!
Τα συγχαρητήριά μου στον μάγειρα!
ta sinharitiria moo ston mayira

MENU GUIDE

αγγινάρες αυγολέμονο	anginares avgolemono	artichokes in egg and lemon sauce
αγγούρι και ντομάτα σαλάτα	angoori ke domata salata	cucumber and tomato salad
αλάτι	alati	salt
αλεύρι καλαμποκιού	alevri kalabokioo	corn flour
αλεύρι σταριού	alevri starioo	wheat flour
αλλαντικά	alandika	sausages, salami, meats
αμύγδαλα	amigthala	almonds
αμυγδαλωτά	amigthalota	macaroons
ανανάς	ananas	pineapple
χυμός ανανά	himos anana	pineapple juice
ανθότυρο	anTHotiro	kind of cottage cheese
αντζούγιες στο λάδι	antsooyies sto lathi	anchovies in oil
αρακάς λαδερός	arakas latheros	peas cooked with tomato and oil
αρακάς σωτέ	arakas sote	peas fried in butter
αρνί μπούτι στη λαδόκολα	arni booti sti lathokola	leg of lamb wrapped in greased foil
αρνί γεμιστό στο φούρνο	arni yemisto sto foorno	oven-cooked stuffed lamb
αρνί εξοχικό	arni exohiko	lamb cooked in greased foil with cheese and spices
αρνί κοκκινιστό	arni kokkinisto	lamb in tomato sauce
αρνί λαδορίγανη στο φούρνο	arni lathoriyani sto foorno	oven-cooked lamb with oil and oregano
αρνί με αρακά	arni me araka	lamb with peas
αρνί με κολοκυθάκια αυγολέμονο	arni me koloki-THakia avgolemono	lamb with courgettes in egg and lemon sauce
αρνί με κριθαράκι	arni me kriTHaraki	lamb with rice-shaped pasta
αρνί με μελιτζάνες	arni me melitzanes	lamb with aubergines
αρνί με μπάμιες	arni me bamies	lamb with okra
αρνί με πατάτες ραγκού	arni me patates ragoo	lamb with potatoes cooked in tomato sauce

αρνί με φασολάκια φρέσκα	arni me fasolakia freska	lamb with runner beans
αρνί με χυλοπίτες	arni me hilopites	lamb with a kind of lasagne
αρνί μπούτι στο φούρνο	arni booti sto foorno	oven-cooked leg of lamb
αρνί μπριζόλες	arni brizoles	lamb chops
αρνί με μακαρόνια	arni me makaronia	lamb with spaghetti
αρνί παιδάκια	arni paithakia	grilled lamb chops
αρνί τας κεμπάπ	arni tas kebab	chopped lamb kebab with tomato sauce
αρνί της κατσαρόλας με πατάτες	arni tis katsarolas me patates	casseroled lamb with potatoes
αρνί της σούβλας	arni tis soovlas	spit-roast lamb
αρνί φρικασέ	arni frikase	lamb fricassee
αστακός με λαδολέμονο	astakos me latholemono	lobster cooked in lemon and oil sauce
αστακός με μαγιονέζα	astakos me mayoneza	lobster with mayonnaise
αστακός βραστός	astakos vrastos	boiled lobster
ατζέμ πιλάφι	atzem pilafi	rice pilaf
αυγά βραστά	avga vrasta	boiled eggs
αυγά βραστά σφιχτά	avga vrasta sfihta	hard-boiled eggs
αυγά γεμιστά	avga yemista	stuffed eggs
αυγά γεμιστά με μαγιονέζα	avga yemista me mayoneza	eggs stuffed with mayonnaise mix
αυγά μάτια	avga matia	fried eggs
αυγά με μανιτάρια	avga me manitaria	mushroom omelette
αυγά με μπέικον	avga me beykon	bacon and eggs
αυγά με ντομάτες	avga me domates	scrambled eggs with tomatoes
αυγά με τυρί	avga me tiri	cheese omelette
αυγά ομελέτα	avga omeleta	plain omelette
αυγά ομελέτα με πατάτες	avga omeleta me patates	omelette with chips
αυγά ποσέ	avga pose	poached eggs
αυγά ώ γκρατέν	avga o graten	eggs au gratin
αυγολέμονο (σούπα)	avgolemono (soopa)	egg and lemon soup
αυγοτάραχο	avgotaraho	roe
αχλάδι χυμός	ahlathi himos	pear juice
αχλαδιά	ahlathia	pears

βακαλάος κροκέτες	vakalaos kroketes	haddock croquettes
βερύκοκκα	verikoka	apricots
τάρτα με βερύκοκκα	tarta me verikoka	apricot tart
χυμός βερύκοκκο	himos verikoko	apricot juice
βούτυρο	vootiro	butter
βούτυρο φυστικιού	vootiro fistikioo	peanut butter
βρασμένος, βραστός	vrasmenos, vrastos	boiled
βυσσινάδα	visingtha	black cherry juice
βύσσινο	visino	cherries
βοδινό βραστό	vothino vrasto	boiled beef
βοδινό ροσμπίφ	vothino rosbif	roast beef
βοδινό φιλέτο	vothino fileto	grilled beef steak
στη σχάρα	sti s-hara	
βοδινό ψητό	vothino psito	roast beef cooked in the
στο φούρνο	sto foorno	oven
βοδινός κιμάς	vothinos kimas	minced beef
βοδινό κορν-μπίφ	vothino korn-bif	corned beef
γάβρος στο φούρνο	gavross sto foorno	small type of fish cooked
με ντομάτα	me domata	in the oven with
		tomato sauce
γάβρος τηγανιτός	gavros tiganitos	fried small fish
γάλα	gala	milk
γάλα αγελάδος με λίπος	gala agelathos me lipos	cow's milk with 1% fat
ένα της εκατό	ena tis ekato	
γάλα εβαπορέ	gala evapore	evaporated milk
γάλα σοκολατούχο	gala sokolatooho	chocolate milk
γάλα συμπηκνωμένο	gala sibiknomeno	sweet evaporated milk
ζαχαρούχο	zaharooho	
γαλακτομπούρεκο	galaktobooreko	cream pie with honey
γαλέος τηγανητός	galeos tiganitos	fried cod with
σκορδαλιά	skorthalia	garlic sauce
γαλλικός καφές	galikos kafes	French (filtered) coffee
γαλοπούλα ψητή στο	galopoola psiti sto	roast turkey
φούρνο	foorno	
γαλοπούλα γεμιστή	galopoola yemisti	stuffed turkey
γαλοπούλα κοκκινιστή	galopoola kokinisti	turkey cooked with
		tomatoes
γαρίδες καναπέ	garithes kanape	shrimp canapés
γαρδούμπα	garthooba	lamb's intestines
		on the spit

γαρίδες βραστές	garithes vrastes	boiled shrimps
γαρίδες κοκτέιλ	garithes kokteyl	shrimp cocktail
γαρίδες πιλάφι	garithes pilafi	shrimp pilaf
γαρνιτούρα με καρότα σωτέ	garnitoora me karota sote	sautéed carrots
γαρνιτούρα με κουνουπίδι σωτέ	garnitoora me kounoupithi sote	sautéed cauliflower
γαρνιτούρα πατάτες	garnitoora patates	potatoes
γαρνιτούρα με σπανάκι σωτέ	garnitoora me spanaki sote	sautéed spinach
γαρνιτούρα φασόλια πράσινα σωτέ	garnitoora fasolia prasina sote	sautéed runner beans
γαρνιτούρα με φασόλια ξερά σωτέ	garnitoora me fasolia xera sote	sautéed butter beans
γιαλατζή ντολμάδες	yalantzi dolmathes	vine leaves stuffed with rice
γιαούρτι αγελάδος άπαχο	yaoorti ayelathos apaho	low-fat cow's yoghurt
γιαούρτι αγελάδος πλήρες	yaoorti ayelathos plires	full-fat cow's yoghurt
γιαούρτι πρόβειο	yaoorti provio	sheep's yoghurt
γιαούρτι φρούτων	yaoorti frooton	fruit yoghurt
γιουβαρλάκια αυγολέμονο	yioovarlakia avgolemono	meatballs with rice in egg and lemon sauce
γιουβαρλάκια με σάλτσα ντομάτας	yioovarlakia me saltsa domatas	meatballs with rice cooked with tomatoes
γιουβέτσι	yoovetsi	oven-cooked lamb with a kind of pasta
γκοφρέττα	gofreta	chocolate wafer
γκρέϊπ φρουτ	'grapefruit'	grapefruit
γκρέϊπ φρουτ χυμός	'grapefruit' himos	grapefruit juice
γλυκό μελιτζανάκι	gliko melitzanaki	aubergine preserve in syrup
γλυκό βύσσινο	gliko visino	cherry preserve in syrup
γλυκό καρυδάκι φρέσκο	gliko karithaki fresko	green walnut preserve in syrup
γλυκό μαστίχα	gliko mastiha	vanilla-flavoured fudge
γλυκό νεραντζάκι	gliko nerantzaki	bitter orange in syrup
γλυκό σύκο φρέσκο	gliko siko fresko	fig preserve in syrup
γλυκό τριαντάφυλλο	gliko triadafilo	dried rose petal preserve

γλώσσα	glosa	sole
γλώσσες τηγανητή	gloses tiganiti	fried sole
γόπα τηγανητή	gopa tiganiti	type of fried fish
γουρουνόπουλο στο φούρνο με πατάτες	gooroonopoolo sto foorno me patates	oven-cooked pork with potatoes
γραβιέρα τυρί	graviera tiri	kind of savoury cheese
γρανίτα από λεμόνι	granita apo lemoni	lemon sorbet
γρανίτα από μπανάνα	granita apo banana	banana sorbet
γρανίτα από πορτοκάλι	granita apo portokali	orange sorbet
γρανίτα από φράουλες	granita apo fraooles	strawberry sorbet
δαμάσκηνα	thamaskina	prunes
δίπλες, τηγανητές	thiples, tiganites	pancakes
εκλαίρ σοκολάτας	ekler sokolatas	chocolate éclair
ελαιόλαδο	eleolatho	olive oil
ελιές	elies	olives
ελληνικός καφές	elinikos kafes	Greek coffee
εντόσθια αρνιού λαδορίγανη	entosthia arnioo lathorigani	lamb's intestines cooked in lemon and oil
εσκαλόπ με ζαμπόν και σάλτσα ντομάτας	eskalop me zabon ke saltsa domatas	escalope of veal with ham and tomato sauce
ζαμπόν	zabon	ham
ζάχαρη μαύρη	zahari mavri	brown sugar
ζάχαρη άσπρη	zahari aspri	white sugar
ζελέ βερύκοκκου	zele verikokkoo	apricot jelly
ζελέ κεράσι	zele kerasi	cherry jelly
ζελέ πορτοκαλιού	zele portokalioo	orange jelly
ζελέ φράουλα	zele fraoola	strawberry jelly
ζυμαρικά	zimarika	pasta
ζωμός κότας/κρέατος/ λαχανικών	zomos kotas/kreatos/ lahanikon	chicken/beef/vegetable stock
ηλιέλαιο	ilieleo	sunflower oil
θαλασσινά	thalassina	seafood
καβούρια ψητά	kavooria psita	grilled crab
κακαβιά	kakavia	fish soup
κακάο	kakao	cocoa
κακάο ρόφημα	kakao rofima	hot chocolate
καλαμαράκια γεμιστά	kalamarakia yemista	stuffed squid
καλαμαράκια τηγανητά	kalamarakia tiganita	fried squid
καλαμποκέλαιο	kalabokeleo	corn oil

καλαμπόκι	kalaboki	corn
καναπέ με ζαμπόν	kanape me zabon	ham canapés
καναπέ με κρέας ψητό	kanape me kreas psito	cooked meat canapés
καναπέ με μαύρο χαβιάρι	kanape me mavro haviari	black caviar canapés
καναπέ με ταραμοσαλάτα	kanape me taramosalata	taramosalata canapés
κανελλόνια γεμιστά	kanelonia yemista	stuffed canelloni
καπαμάς αρνί	kapamas arni	lamb cooked in spices and tomato sauce
καραβίδες	karavithes	prawns
καραμέλες	karameles	sweets
καρμπονάρα	karbonara	spaghetti carbonara
καρότα	karota	carrots
καρπούζι	karpoozi	watermelon
καρύδα	karitha	coconut
καρύδια	karithia	walnuts
καρυδόπιττα	karithopita	cake with nuts and syrup
κασέρι	kaseri	type of Greek cheese
κάστανα	kastana	chestnuts
κάστανα γκλασέ	kastana glase	glazed chestnuts
καταΐφι	kataifi	sweet with honey and nuts
καφές βαρύς γλυκός	kafes varis glikos	sweet Greek coffee
καφές με γάλα	kafes me gala	coffee with milk
καφές μέτριος	kafes metrios	medium sweet Greek coffee
κέϊκ κανέλλας	keik kanelas	cinnamon cake
κέϊκ με αμύγδαλα	keik me amigdala	almond cake
κέϊκ με καρύδια και σταφίδες	keik me karithia ke stafithes	nut and sultana cake
κέϊκ σοκολάτας	keik sokolatas	chocolate cake
κέϊκ φρούτων	keik frooton	fruit cake
κεράσια	kerasia	cherries
κέτσαπ	ketsap	ketchup
κέφαλος	kefalos	mullet
κεφαλοτύρι	kefalotiri	type of Greek parmesan-style cheese
κεφτέδες τηγανητοί	keftethes tiganiti	fried meatballs
κεφτέδες με σάλτσα	keftethes me saltsa	meatballs in tomato sauce

κεφτέδες στο φούρνο	keftethes sto foorno	oven-cooked meatballs
κόκα κόλα	koka kola	Coca Cola®
κοκορέτσι	kokoretsi	spit-roast lamb's intestines
κολιοί ψητοί	koli-i psiti	fried mackerel
κολοκυθάκια γεμιστά με ρύζι	kolokiTHakia yemista me rizi	courgettes stuffed with rice and mince
κολοκυθάκια λαδερά	kolokiTHakia lathera	courgettes cooked in oil
κολοκυθάκια σαλάτα	kolokiTHakia salata	courgette salad
κολοκυθάκια τηγανητά	kolokiTHakia tiganita	fried courgettes
κολοκυθοκεφτέδες	kolokiTHokeftethes	fried courgette balls
κολοκυθοτυρόπιττα	kolokiTHotiropita	courgette and cheese pie
κολοκυθάκια γεμιστά με κιμά	kolokiTHakia yemista me kima	courgettes stuffed with minced meat
κολοκυθάκια με πατάτες	kolokiTHakia me patates	courgettes with potatoes
κολοκυθάκια μουσακάς	kolokiTHakia mousakas	courgettes with minced meat and béchamel sauce
κολοκυθάκια παπουτσάκι	kolokiTHakia papootsaki	courgettes with minced meat and onions
κομπόστα με βερύκοκκα	komposta me verikoka	apricot compôte
κομπόστα με μήλα	komposta me mila	apple compôte
κομπόστα με ροδάκινα	komposta me rothakina	peach compôte
κορν φλέϊκς	korn fleiks	corn flakes
κότα βραστή	kota vrasti	boiled chicken
κότα γεμιστή	kota yemisti	stuffed chicken
κότα κοκκινιστή	kota kokkinisti	chicken in tomato sauce
κότα ψητή στο φούρνο	kota psiti sto foorno	roast chicken
κότα ψητή σούβλας	kota psiti soovlas	spit-roast chicken
κότα ψητή της κατσαρόλας	kota psiti tis katsarolas	roast chicken in the pot
κοτολέτες αρνίσιες πανέ	kotolete arnisies pane	lamb cutlets

κοτολέτες μοσχαρίσιες πανέ	kotoletes mos-harisies pane	veal cutlets
κοτόπιττα	kotopita	chicken pie
κοτόπουλο γιουβέτσι με χυλοπίττες	kotopoolo yioovetsi me hilopites	chicken with a kind of pasta
κοτόπουλο με μπάμιες	kotopoolo me bamies	chicken with okra
κοτόπουλο με μπιζέλια	kotopoolo me bizelia	chicken with peas
κοτόπουλο πανέ	kotopoolo pane	breaded chicken
κοτόπουλο πιλάφι	kotopoolo pilafi	chicken pilaf
κοτόσουπα	kotosoopa	chicken soup
κουκιά λαδερά	kookia lathera	broad beans in tomato sauce
κουλούρια κανέλλας/ με σουσάμι	koolooria kanelas/ me soosami	cinnamon/sesame biscuits
κουνέλι με σάλτσα	kooneli me saltsa	rabbit with tomato sauce
κουνέλι στιφάδο	kooneli stifatho	rabbit with onions
κουνουπίδι βραστό σαλάτα	koonoopithi vrasto salata	boiled cauliflower salad
κουραμπιέδες με αμύγδαλο	koorabiethes me amigthalo	shortbread with nuts and icing sugar
κράκερς αλμυρά	krakers almira	savoury crackers
κρασί	krasi	wine
κρασί άσπρο	krasi aspro	white wine
κρασί κόκκινο	krasi kokino	red wine
κρασί μαυροδάφνη	krasi mavrothafni	sweet red wine
κρασί ρετσίνα	krasi retsina	dry white Greek wine
κρασί ροζέ	krasi roze	rosé
κρέας με αντίδια αυγολέμονο	kreas me antithia avgolemono	beef with endives in egg and lemon sauce
κρέας με φασόλια ξερά	kreas me fasolia xera	beef with butter beans
κρεατόπιττες	kreatopites	minced meat pies
κρέμα καραμελέ	krema karamele	crème caramel
κρέμα με μήλα	krema me mila	apples with cream
κρέμα με μπανάνες	krema me bananes	bananas with cream
κρεμμυδάκια φρέσκα	kremithakia freska	spring onions
κρεμμύδια	kremithia	onions

κρεμμυδόσουπα	kremithosoopa	onion soup
κροκέτες απο κρέας	kroketes apo kreas	meat croquettes
κροκέτες με αυγά και τυρί	kroketes me avga ke tiri	croquettes with egg and cheese
κροκέτες με μπακαλιάρο	kroketes me bakaliaro	cod croquettes
κροκέτες με πατάτα	kroketes me patata	potato croquettes
κρουασάν	krooasan	croissants
κυδωνόπαστο	kithonopasto	thick quince jelly
κωκ	kok	cream cake with chocolate topping
λαγός με σάλτσα	lagos me saltsa	hare in tomato sauce
λαγός στιφάδο	lagos stifatho	hare with onions
λάδι	lathi	oil
λαζάνια	lazania	lasagne
λαχανάκια Βρυξελλών	lahanakia vrixelon	Brussels sprouts
λαχανάκια μικτά	lahanika mikta	mixed vegetables
λάχανο	lahano	cabbage
λάχανο κόκκινο	lahano kokino	red cabbage
λάχανο ντολμάδες αυγολέμονο	lahano dolmathes avgolemono	stuffed cabbage leaves in egg and lemon sauce
λάχανο ντολμάδες με σάλτσα ντομάτας	lahano dolmathes me saltsa domatas	stuffed vine leaves in tomato sauce
λάχανοσαλάτα	lahanosalata	cabbage salad
λεμόνι	lemoni	lemon
χυμός λεμονιού	himos lemonioo	lemon juice
λιθρίνι ψητό	liтHrini psito	grilled mullet
λουκάνικα βραστά	lookanika vrasta	boiled sausages
λουκάνικα καπνιστά στη σχάρα	lookanika kapnista sti s-hara	smoked sausages on the grill
λουκάνικα τηγανητά	lookanika tiganita	fried sausages
λουκουμάδες	lookoomathes	doughnuts
λουκούμια	lookoomia	Turkish delight
μαγειρίτσα	mayiritsa	Easter soup with lamb's intestines
μαγιά	mayia	yeast
μαγιονέζα	mayoneza	mayonnaise
μαϊντανός	maidanos	parsley

μακαρονάκι κοφτό	makaronaki kofto	macaroni
μακαρόνια με κιμά	makaronia me kima	spaghetti Bolognese
μακαρόνια με φρέσκο βούτυρο και παρμεζάνα	makaronia me fresko vootiro ke parmezana	spaghetti with fresh butter and parmesan cheese
μακαρόνια παστίτσιο με κιμά	makaronia pastitsio me kima	spaghetti with rice and béchamel sauce
μανιτάρια	manitaria	mushrooms
μανιτάρια τηγανητά	manitaria tiganita	fried mushrooms
μανταρίνι	madarini	tangerine
μαργαρίνη	margarini	margarine
μαρίδες τηγανητές	marithes tiganites	small fried fish
μαρμελάδα βερύκοκκο	marmelatha verikoko	apricot jam
μαρμελάδα πορτοκάλι	marmelatha portokali	orange jam
μαρμελάδα ροδάκινο	marmelatha rothakino	peach jam
μαρμελάδα φράουλα	marmelatha fraoola	strawberry jam
μαρούλια σαλάτα	maroolia salata	lettuce salad
μέλι	meli	honey
μελιτζάνες γιαχνί	melitzanes yahni	aubergines in tomato and onions
μελιτζάνες παπουτσάκι	melitzanes papootsaki	aubergines cooked with minced meat and tomato
μελιτζάνες γεμιστές με κιμά	melitzanes yemistes me kima	aubergines stuffed with minced meat
μελιτζάνες ιμάμ μπαϊλντί	melitzanes imam baildi	aubergines in garlic and tomato
μελιτζάνες μουσακάς	melitzanes moosakas	aubergines in minced meat, potato and béchamel sauce
μελιτζάνες τηγανητές	melitzanes tiganites	fried aubergines
μελιτζάνοσαλάτα	melitzanosalata	aubergine salad
μελομακάρονα	melomakarona	sweet cakes with cinnamon, nuts and syrup
μήλα	mila	apples
μήλα γεμιστά	mila yemista	stuffed apples with cinnamon
μηλόπιττα	milopita	apple pie

μηλοχυμός	milohimos	apple juice
μοσχάρι βραστό	mos-hari vrasto	veal stew
μοσχάρι κοκκινιστό	mos-hari kokkinisto	veal in tomato sauce
μοσχάρι με κριθαράκι	mos-hari me kriTHaraki	veal with rice-shaped pasta
μοσχάρι με μελιτζάνες	mos-hari me melitzanes	veal with aubergines
μοσχάρι με μπάμιες	mos-hari me bamies	veal with okra
μοσχάρι με πατάτες	mos-hari me patates	veal with potatoes
μοσχάρι με πατάτες στο φούρνο	mos-hari me patates sto foorno	veal with potatoes cooked in the oven
μοσχάρι με πουρέ	mos-hari me poore	veal with mashed potatoes
μοσχάρι ροσμπίφ	mos-hari rosbif	roast beef
μοσχάρι με αρακά	mos-hari me araka	veal with peas
μοσχάρι σνίτσελ με πατάτες τηγανές	mos-hari snitzel me patates tiganites	steak and chips
μοσχάρι σνίτσελ με πουρέ	mos-hari snitzel me poore	steak with mashed potatoes
μοσχαρίσιος κιμάς	mos-harisios kimas	minced beef
μουσακά	moosaka	moussaka
μουσακάς με πατάτες	moosakas me patates	potatoes with minced meat and béchamel sauce
μουστοκούλουρα	moostokooloora	kind of Greek biscuits
μουστάρδα	moostartha	mustard
μπακαλιάρος πλακί	bakaliaros plaki	salted cod cooked in tomato sauce
μπακαλιάρος τηγανητός	bakaliaros tiganitos	fried salt cod
μπακλαβάς	baclavas	layers of filo pastry with nuts and syrup
μπάμιες λαδερές	bamies latheres	okra with tomato in oil
μπανάνα	banana	banana
μπαρμπούνια πανέ	barboonia pane	breaded red mullet
μπεζέδες	bezethes	meringues with cream
μπέϊκον καπνιστό	beikon kapnisto	smoked bacon
μπεσαμέλ σάλτσα	besamel saltsa	béchamel sauce
μπισκότα σοκολάτας	biskota sokolatas	chocolate biscuits
μπισκοτάκια αλμυρά	biskotakia almira	savoury biscuits
μπιφτέκι	bifteki	grilled meatballs
μπον φιλέ	bon file	fillet steak

μπουγάτσα γλυκιά	*boogatsa glikia*	puff pastry with cream filling and icing sugar
μπουρεκάκια	*boorekakia*	cheese or mince pies
μπριάμι με κολοκυθάκια	*briami me kolokiᴛʜakia*	courgettes cooked with potatoes in the oven
μπριζόλες βωδινές στη σχάρα	*brizoles vothines sti s-hara*	grilled T-bone steak
μπριζόλες στο τηγάνι	*brizoles sto tigani*	fried T-bone steak
μπριζόλες χοιρινές	*brizoles hirines*	pork chops
μπρόκολο	*brokolo*	broccoli
μπύρα	*bira*	beer
μυαλά πανέ	*miala pane*	breaded cow's brains
μύδια τηγανητά	*mithia tiganita*	fried mussels
νες καφέ	*nes kafe*	any instant coffee
νεφρά ψητά/τηγανητά	*nefra psita /tiganita*	grilled/fried kidneys
ντολμάδες αυγολέμονο με κιμά	*dolmathes avgolemono me kima*	vine leaves stuffed with rice and minced meat in egg and lemon sauce
ντολμάδες γιαλαντζή	*dolmathes yialantzi*	stuffed vine leaves with rice
ντοματόσουπα	*domatosoopa*	tomato soup
χυμός ντομάτα	*himos domata*	tomato juice
ντομάτες γεμιστές με κιμά	*domates yemistes me kima*	tomatoes stuffed with rice and minced meat
ντοματοσαλάτα	*domatosalata*	tomato salad
ντομάτα	*domata*	tomato
ντομάτες γεμιστές με ρύζι	*domates yemistes me rizi*	stuffed tomatoes with rice
ντόνατς	*donats*	doughnuts
ξηροί καρποί	*xiri karpi*	all types of nuts
ξιφίας	*xifias*	sword fish
ξύδι	*xithi*	vinegar
ομελέτα	*omeleta*	omelette
ομελέτα με λουκάνικα	*omeleta me lookanika*	omelette with sausages
ορεκτικά	*orektika*	hors d'oeuvres
ούζο	*oozo*	ouzo
παγωτό κοκτέϊλ	*pagoto kokteil*	ice cream cocktail
παγωτό κρέμα	*pagoto krema*	vanilla ice cream
παγωτό βερύκοκκο	*pagoto verikoko*	apricot ice cream

παγωτό με σαντυγί	pagoto me sandiyi	ice cream with whipped cream
παγωτό μόκκα	pagoto moka	coffee ice cream
παγωτό μπανάνα	pagoto banana	banana ice cream
παγωτό παρφαί	pagoto parfe	ice cream parfait
παγωτό πραλίνα	pagoto pralina	praline ice cream
παγωτό σοκολάτα	pagoto sokolata	chocolate ice cream
παγωτό φράουλα	pagoto fraoola	strawberry ice cream
παγωτό φυστίκι	pagoto fistiki	pistachio ice cream
πάπρικα	paprika	paprika
πάστα αμυγδάλου	pasta amigdaloo	almond gâteau
πάστα κορμός	pasta kormos	chocolate log
πάστα νουγκατίν	pasta noogatin	cream gâteau
πάστα σοκολατίνα	pasta sokolatina	chocolate gâteau
πάστα φράουλα	pasta fraoola	strawberry gâteau
παστίτσιο λαζάνια	pastitsio lazania	lasagne
παστίτσιο μακαρόνια με κιμά	pastitsio makaronia me kima	macaroni and minced meat cooked in the oven with béchamel
πατάτες γαρνιτούρα	patates garnitoora	potatoes
πατάτες γιαχνί	patates yiahni	potatoes cooked with onion and tomato
πατάτες με κολοκυθάκια στο φούρνο	patates ke kolokiTHakia sto foorno	potatoes, courgettes and tomatoes cooked in the oven
πατάτες με κολοκύθια μουσακάς	patates ke kolokiTHia moosakas	potatoes with courgettes, mince and cheese sauce
πατάτες πουρέ	patates poore	mashed potatoes
πατάτες σουφλέ	patates soofle	potato soufflé
πατάτες στο φούρνο ριγανάτες	patates sto foorno riganates	potatoes baked in the oven with oregano, lemon and olive oil
πατάτες τηγανητές	patates tiganites	chips/French fries
πατάτες τσιπς	patates tsips	potato crisps
πατατοσαλάτα	patatosalata	potato salad
πατζάρια	patzaria	beetroots
πατσάς σούπα	patsas soopa	tripe soup
πεπόνι	peponi	melon
πέστροφα ψητή	pestrofa psiti	grilled trout
πηχτή	pihti	brawn

πιλάφι με γαρίδες	*pilafi me garithes*	shrimp pilaf
πιλάφι με μύδια	*pilafi me mithia*	rice with mussels
πιλάφι με σάλτσα ντομάτα	*pilafi me saltsa domata*	rice with tomato sauce
πιλάφι τας-κεμπάπ	*pilafi tas-kebab*	rice with cubes of beef in tomato sauce
πιπέρι	*piperi*	pepper
πιπεριές γεμιστές με ρύζι/κιμά	*piperies yemistes me rizi/kima*	peppers stuffed with rice/mince
πιπεριές πράσινες/ κόκκινες	*piperies prasines/kokines*	green/red peppers
πιπεριές τηγανητές	*piperies tiganites*	fried peppers
πιροσκί	*piroski*	mince or sausage rolls
πίτσα με ζαμπόν	*pitsa me zabon*	ham pizza
πίτσα με μανιτάρια	*pitsa me manitaria*	mushroom pizza
πίτσα με ντομάτα και τυρί	*pitsa me domata ke tiri*	cheese and tomato pizza
πίτσα σπέσιαλ	*pitsa spesial*	special pizza
πίττα με κιμά	*pita me kima*	minced meat pie
πορτοκαλάδα	*portokalatha*	orange juice
πορτοκάλι	*portokali*	orange
χυμός πορτοκάλι	*himos portokali*	orange juice
πουτίγκα με ανανά	*pootiga me anana*	pineapple pudding
πουτίγκα με καρύδια	*pootiga me karithia*	pudding with walnuts
πουτίγκα με σταφίδες	*pootiga me stafithes*	sultana pudding
πρασσόπιττα	*prasopita*	leek pie
πράσσα	*prasa*	leeks
παρμεζάνα	*parmezana*	parmesan cheese
ραβιόλια	*raviolia*	ravioli
ραβανί	*ravani*	very sweet sponge cake
ρίγανη	*rigani*	oregano
ροδάκινα	*rothakina*	peaches
ροσμπίφ αρνί μοσχάρι	*rozbif arni mos-hari*	roast beef, veal or lamb
ρυζόγαλο	*rizogalo*	rice pudding
ρώσικη σαλάτα	*rosiki salata*	vegetable salad
σαλάμι	*salami*	salami
σαλάτα	*salata*	salad
σαλάτα αμπελοφάσουλα	*salata abelofasoola*	runner bean salad
σαλάτα με κουνουπίδι βραστό	*salata me koonoopithi vrasto*	boiled cauliflower salad

σαλάτα με μαρούλια	salata me maroolia	lettuce salad
σαλάτα με ντομάτες και αγγούρια	salata me domates ke agooria	tomato and cucumber salad
σαλάτα με ντομάτες και πιπεριές	salata me domates ke piperies	tomato and green pepper salad
σαλάτα με σπαράγγια	salata me sparagia	asparagus salad
σαλάτα με φασόλια ξερά	salata me fasolia xera	butter bean salad
σαλάτα με χόρτα βρασμένα	salata me horta vrasmena	chicory salad
σαλάτα χωριάτικη	salata horiatiki	Greek salad – tomatoes, cucumber, feta cheese, peppers and olives
σαλιγκάρια	saligaria	snails
σάλτσα μπεσαμέλ	saltsa besamel	béchamel sauce
σάλτσα ντομάτα	saltsa domata	tomato sauce
σαμάλι	samali	semolina cake with honey
σαντιγή	sandiyi	whipped cream
σαρδέλλες λαδιού	sartheles lathioo	sardines in oil
σέλινο	selino	celery
σιμιγδάλη	simigthali	semolina
σιρόπι	siropi	syrup
σκορδαλιά με ψωμί	skorthalia me psomi	thick garlic sauce with bread
σκόρδο	skortho	garlic
σοκολάτα	sokolata	chocolate
σοκολατάκια	sokolatgkia	milk chocolates
σολομός καπνιστός	solomos kapnistos	smoked salmon
σουβλάκι καλαμάκι	soovlaki kalamaki	shish kebab
σουβλάκι ντονέρ με πίτα	soovlaki doner me pita	doner kebab with pitta bread
σουβλάκια απο κρέας μοσχαρίσιο	soovlakia apo kreas mos-harisio	veal kebab
σουβλάκια απο κρέας αρνίσιο	soovlakia apo kreas arnisio	lamb kebab
σουβλάκια απο κρέας χοιρινό	soovlakia apo kreas hirino	pork kebab
σούπα ρεβύθια	soopa revithia	chickpea soup
σούπα τραχανάς	soopa trahanas	milk broth with flour
σούπα φακές	soopa fakes	lentil soup

σούπα ψάρι/ ψαρόσουπα αυγολέμονο	soopa psari/psarosoopa avgolemono	fish soup with egg and lemon
σουπιές τηγανητές	soopies tiganites	fried cuttlefish
σουσάμι	soosami	sesame
σουτζουκάκια	sootzookakia	spicy meatballs in red sauce
σουφλέ με ζαμπόν	soofle me zabon	ham soufflé
σπαγέτο με φρέσκο βούτυρο και παρμεζάνα	spageto me fresko vootiro ke parmezana	spaghetti with fresh butter and parmesan cheese
σπαράγγια σαλάτα	sparangia salata	asparagus salad
σπληνάντερο	splinandero	intestines stuffed with spleen
σταφίδες	stafithes	raisins
σταφιδόψωμο	stafithopsomo	bread with raisins
σταφύλι χυμός	stafili himos	grape juice
σταφύλια	stafilia	grapes
στιφάδο	stifatho	chopped meat in onions
στρείδια	strithia	oysters
σύκα	sika	figs
συκωτάκια μαρινάτα	sikotakia marinata	liver cooked in rosemary
συκωτάκια πιλάφι	sikotakia pilafi	liver pilaf
συκωτάκια στη σχάρα	sikotakia sti s-hara	grilled liver
συκωτάκια τηγανητά	sikotakia tiganita	fried liver
συναγρίδα ψητή	sinagritha psiti	grilled sea bream
σφυρίδα βραστή	sfiritha vrasti	boiled pike
ταραμοκεφτέδες	taramokeftethes	roe pâté balls with spices
ταραμοσαλάτα	taramosalata	roe pâté
τάρτα με κεράσια	tarta me kerasia	cherry tart
τάρτα με κρέμα και αμύγδαλα	tarta me krema ke amigthala	cream and almond tart
τάρτα με κρέμα και καρύδια	tarta me krema ke karithia	cream and walnut tart
τάρτα με φράουλες	tarta me fraooles	strawberry tart
τάρτα μήλου	tarta miloo	apple tart
τας-κεμπάπ	tas kebab	spicy lamb cutlets
τας-κεμπάπ πιλάφι	tas kebab pilafi	spicy lamb cutlets pilaf
τζατζίκι	tzatziki	yoghurt, cucumber, garlic, dried mint and olive oil
τηγανητός	tiganitos	fried

MENU GUIDE

τηγανήτες	tiganites	pancakes
τονοσαλάτα	tonosalata	tuna salad
τόνος	tonos	tuna
τοστ κλαμπ	tost klab	toasted club sandwich
τοστ με αυγό/ζαμπόν/ τυρί/κοτόπουλο	tost me avgo/zabon/ tiri/kotopoolo	toasted sandwich with egg/ham/cheese/chicken
τοστ με κρέας/ μπιφτέκι	tost me kreas/bifteki	toasted sandwich with meat/hamburger
τούρτα αμυγδάλου	toorta amigdaloo	almond gâteau
τούρτα κρέμα με φράουλες	toorta krema me fraooles	gâteau with strawberries and cream
τούρτα μόκκα	toorta moka	coffee gâteau
τούρτα νουγκατίνα	toorta noogatina	nougat gâteau
τούρτα σαντυγί	toorta sandiyi	whipped cream gâteau
τούρτα σοκολάτας	toorta sokolatas	chocolate gâteau
τρουφάκια	troofakia	small chocolate balls
τσάι	tsai	tea
τσιπούρες ψητές	tsipoores psites	roast flatfish
τσίπουρο	tsipooro	kind of ouzo
τσουρέκια	tsoorekia	sweet Easter bread with fresh butter
τυρί	tiri	cheese
τυρόπιττα	tiropita	cheese pie
τυροπιττάκια	tiropitakia	small cheese pies
φάβα	fava	continental lentils
φασολάδα	fasolatha	thick bean soup
φασολάκια λαδερά	fasolakia lathera	runner beans in oil
φασολάκια φρέσκα γιαχνί	fasolakia freska yahni	runner beans with onions and tomato
φασολάκια φρέσκα σαλάτα	fasolakia freska salata	runner bean salad
φασόλια γίγαντες γιαχνί	fasolia yigades yahni	butter beans with onion and tomato
φασόλια γίγαντες στο φούρνο	fasolia yigades sto foorno	oven-cooked butter beans
φέτα	feta	feta cheese
φιλέ μινιόν	file minion	thin fillet steak
φιλέτο	fileto	fillet steak
φοντάν αμυγδάλου	fodan amigthaloo	almond sweets
φοντάν απο καρύδια	fodan apo karithia	walnut sweets

φοντάν ινδικής καρύδας	*fodan inthikis karithas*	coconut sweet
φουντούκι	*foodooki*	hazelnut
φράουλες	*fraooles*	strawberries
φράουλες μέ σαντυγί	*fraooles me sandiyi*	strawberries with whipped cream
φρικασέ αρνί	*frikase arni*	lamb cooked in lettuce with cream sauce
φρουί-γκλασέ	*frooi-glase*	dried assorted fruits with sugar
φρουτοσαλάτα	*frootosalata*	fruit salad
φρυγανιές	*friganies*	French toast
φύλλο πίττας	*filo pitas*	thin pastry
φυστίκια	*fistikia*	peanuts
φυστίκια Αιγίνης	*fistikia eyinis*	pistachios
χαβιάρι	*haviari*	caviar
χαλβάς	*halvas*	halva, sweet made from sesame seeds and nuts
χάμπουργκερ	*hamboorger*	hamburger
χοιρινό με σέλινο	*hirino me selino*	pork casserole with celery
χοιρινό παστό	*hirino pasto*	salted pork
χοιρινό σούβλας	*hirino soovlas*	pork on the spit
χοιρινό στη σχάρα	*hirino sti s-hara*	grilled pork
χοιρινό φούρνου με πατάτες	*hirino foornoo me patates*	roast pork with potatoes
χόρτα βρασμένα σαλάτα	*horta vrasmena salata*	boiled chicory salad
χορτόσουπα	*hortosoopa*	vegetable soup
χταπόδι βραστό	*htapothi vrasto*	boiled octopus
χταπόδι κρασάτο	*htapothi krasato*	octopus in wine
χταπόδι με μακαρονάκι	*htapothi me makaronaki*	octopus with macaroni
χταπόδι πιλάφι	*htapothi pilafi*	octopus pilaf
χταπόδι στιφάδο	*htapothi stifatho*	octopus with small onions
χυλοπίττες με βούτυρο και τυρί	*hilopites me vootiro ke tiri*	tagliatelle with butter and cheese
χυλοπίττες με κοτόπουλο	*hilopites me kotopoolo*	tagliatelle with chicken
χυλοπίττες με κιμά	*hilopites me kima*	tagliatelle with mince sauce

MENU GUIDE

χυμός	*himos*	juice
χυμός ντομάτας	*himos domatas*	tomato juice
χωριάτικη σαλάτα	*horiatiki salata*	Greek salad – tomatoes, cucumber, feta cheese, peppers and olives
ψάρι βραστό μαγιονέζα	*psari vrasto mayoneza*	steamed fish with mayonnaise
ψάρια γλώσσες βραστές με αυγολέμονο	*psaria gloses vrastes me avgolemono*	steamed sole with oil and lemon
ψάρια μαρινάτα	*psaria marinata*	marinated fish
ψάρια τηγανητά	*psaria tiganita*	fried fish
ψάρια ψητά στη σχάρα	*psaria psita sti s-hara*	charcoal-grilled fish
ψαρόσουπα	*psarosoopa*	fish soup
ψητός	*psitos*	grilled
ψωμί άσπρο/μαύρο	*psomi aspro/mavro*	white/brown bread
ψωμί για τοστ	*psomi ya tost*	sliced bread

SHOPPING

The main thing to remember about shopping in Greece is that most shops will be closed for quite a long period during the middle of the day when the sun is at its hottest. Small village shops will tend to be open for 12 hours or more a day, but they are liable to be closed from 1 pm until 4 pm. Shops in the towns open from 8 am until 2.30 pm and from 5 pm until 8.30 pm. Shops close on Sundays and public holidays, with the exception of tourist-orientated shops, which will tend to be open all week and until later hours in the evening. The **periptero** (street kiosk), found in every town, is usually open from 7 am to 11 pm and sells items such as cigarettes, sweets, bus tickets, stamps and postcards, as well as a lot of small items that you might need on a day-to-day basis – and they usually have a public telephone as well.

USEFUL WORDS AND PHRASES

baker	ο φούρναρης	o foornaris
bookshop	το βιβλιοπωλείο	to vivliopolio
butcher	ο χασάπης	o hasapis
buy (verb)	αγοράζω	agorazo
cake shop	το ζαχαροπλαστείο	to zaharoplastio
cheap	φτηνό	ftino
chemist	το φαρμακείο	to farmakio
fashion	η μόδα	i motha
fishmonger	το ψαράδικο	to psarathiko
florist	το ανθοπωλείο	to anthopolio
greengrocer	το μανάβικο	to manaviko
grocer	το μπακάλικο	to bakaliko
ironmonger	το σιδεράδικο	to sitherathiko
menswear	τα ανδρικά	ta anthrika
newsagent	το εφημεριδοπωλείο	to efimerithopolio
pharmacy	το φαρμακείο	to farmakio
receipt	η απόδειξη	i apothixi

record shop	το δισκάδικο	*to thiskathiko*
sales	οι εκπτώσεις	*i ekptosis*
shoe shop	το υποδηματοπωλείο	*to ipothimatopolio*
shop	το μαγαζί	*to magazi*
go shopping	πάω για ψώνια	*pao ya psonia*
souvenir shop	τουριστικά είδη	*tooristika ithi*
special offer	η τιμή ευκαιρίας	*i timi efkerias*
to spend	ξοδεύω	*xothevo*
stationer	το βιβλιοπωλείο	*to vivliopolio*
supermarket	το σούπερ-μάρκετ	*to 'supermarket'*
tailor	ο ράφτης	*o raftis*
till	το ταμείο	*to tamio*
toy shop	το κατάστημα παιχνιδιών	*to katastima pehnithion*
travel agent	το γραφείο ταξειδίων	*to grafio taxithion*
women's wear	τα γυναικεία	*ta yinekia*

I'd like …
Θα ήθελα …
THa iTHela

Do you have …?
Εχετε …;
ehete

How much is this?
Πόσο κάνει αυτό;
poso kani afto

Where is the … department?
Που είναι το τμήμα των …;
poo ine to tmima ton

Do you have any more of these?
Έχετε κι'αλλα απ'αυτά;
ehete kiala apafta

I'd like to change this, please
Θα ήθελα να το αλλάξω αυτό, παρακαλώ
THa iτHela na to alaxo afto, parakalo

Have you anything cheaper?
Έχετε τίποτα φτηνότερο;
ehete tipota ftinotero

Have you anything larger?
Έχετε κανένα μεγαλύτερο;
ehete kanena megalitero

Have you anything smaller?
Έχετε κανένα μικρότερο;
ehete kanena mikrotero

Does it come in other colours?
Το έχετε σε άλλα χρώματα;
to ehete se ala hromata

Could you wrap it for me?
Μου το τυλίγετε;
moo to tiliyete

Can I have a receipt?
Μου δίνετε μία απόδειξη;
moo thinete mia apothixi

Can I have a bag, please?
Μου δίνετε μία σακούλα, παρακαλώ;
moo thinete mia sakoola, parakalo

Can I try it (them) on?
Μπορώ να το (τα) δοκιμάσω;
boro na to (ta) thokimaso

Where do I pay?
Πού πληρώνω;
poo plir<u>o</u>no

I'm just looking
Απλώς κοιτάζω
apl<u>o</u>s kit<u>a</u>zo

I'll come back later
Θα επιστρέψω αργότερα
ΤΗα epistr<u>e</u>pso arg<u>o</u>tera

THINGS YOU'LL SEE

αθλητικά	*aΤΗlitik<u>a</u>*	sports shop
αλλαντικά	*alandik<u>a</u>*	salami, sausages, ham, etc
ανδρικά	*andrik<u>a</u>*	menswear
ανθοπωλείο	*anΤΗopol<u>i</u>o*	florist
αντίκες	*and<u>i</u>kes*	antiques
αρτοποιείο	*artopi-<u>i</u>o*	bakery
βιβλιοπωλείο	*vivliopol<u>i</u>o*	bookshop
γλυκά	*glik<u>a</u>*	cakes
γούνες	*g<u>oo</u>nes*	furs
γραφείο ταξειδίων	*graf<u>i</u>o taxith<u>i</u>on*	travel agency
γυναικεία	*yinek<u>i</u>a*	women's wear
δεν σιδερώνεται	*then sither<u>o</u>nete*	do not iron
δίσκοι, κασσέτες	*th<u>i</u>ski, kas<u>e</u>tes*	records, cassettes
δωδεκάδα	*thothek<u>a</u>tha*	dozen
είδη γραφείου	*<u>i</u>thi graf<u>i</u>oo*	office suppliers
είδη εξοχής	*<u>i</u>thi exoh<u>i</u>s*	holiday articles
ειδική προσφορά	*ithik<u>i</u> prosfor<u>a</u>*	special offer
είσοδος ελευθέρα	*<u>i</u>sothos elefΤΗ<u>e</u>ra*	admission free
εκπτώσεις	*ekpt<u>o</u>sis*	sales
ευκαιρία	*efker<u>i</u>a*	bargain

→

72

εφημερίδες	efimerithes	newspapers
ζαχαροπλαστείο	zaharoplastio	cake shop
ηλεκτρικά είδη	ilektrika ithi	electrical goods
ιχθυοπωλείο	ihтнiopolio	fishmonger
καλλυντικά	kalindika	perfume and cosmetics
κατεψυγμένα	katepsigmena	frozen food
καφές	kafes	coffee
κοσμηματοπωλείο	kosmimatopolio	jewellery
κρεατοπωλείο	kreatopolio	butcher
λαχανικά	lahanika	vegetables
λίρα Αγγλίας	lira Anglias	pound sterling
μόδα	motha	fashion
παιδικά	pethika	children's wear
παιχνίδια	pehnithia	toys
παντοπωλείο	pandopolio	groceries
περιοδικά	periothika	magazines
ποιότητα	piotita	quality
ποτοπωλείο	potopolio	off-licence
ραφείο	rafio	tailor's
σελφ-σέρβις	'self-service'	self-service
σιδηρουργείο	sithirooryio	ironmonger's
τιμή	timi	price
τμήμα	tmima	department
το κιλό	to kilo	a kilo
τσάι	tsai	tea
υποδήματα	ipothimata	shoes
φρούτα	froota	fruit
φτηνό	ftino	cheap
φωτογραφείο	fotografio	camera shop
χαλιά	halia	carpets
ψιλικά	psilika	small shop

THINGS YOU'LL HEAR

Exipiretiste?
Are you being served?

Ehete psila?
Have you anything smaller? (money)

Lipame, mas teliose
I'm sorry, we're out of stock

Parakalo parte ena karotsaki/kalaTHi
Please take a trolley/basket

Afta ehoome mono
This is all we have

Then epistrefoome hrimata
We cannot give cash refunds

AT THE HAIRDRESSER

There are two types of hairdresser in Greece: the traditional ΚΟΥΡΕΙΟ (barber's) which is only for men and where you can also have a shave, and the ΚΟΜΜΩΤΗΡΙΟ (hairdresser's) which is for both men and women. They are usually open Monday and Wednesday from 8 am to 2 pm; Tuesday, Thursday and Friday from 8 am to 2 pm and then from 5–8.30 pm; and on Saturday from 8 am to 4 pm.

USEFUL WORDS AND PHRASES

appointment	το ραντεβού	to randevoo
beard	τα γένια	ta yenia
blond	ξανθιά	xanTHia
brush	η βούρτσα	i voortsa
comb	η τσατσάρα	i tsatsara
conditioner	το κοντίσιονερ	to 'conditioner'
curlers	τα μπικουτί	ta bikooti
curly	σγουρά	sgoora
dark	μαύρα	mavra
gel	ο ζελές	o zeles
hair	τα μαλλιά	ta malia
haircut	το κούρεμα	to koorema
hairdresser	η κομμώτρια	i komotria
hairdryer	το πιστολάκι	to pistolaki
highlights	η μες	i mes
long	μακριά	makria
moustache	το μουστάκι	to moostaki
parting	η χωρίστρα	i horistra
perm	η περμανάντ	i permanant
shampoo	το σαμπουάν	to sampooan
shave	το ξύρισμα	to xirisma
shaving foam	ο αφρός ξυρίσματος	o afros xirismatos
short	κοντά	konda
styling mousse	η μπριγιαντίνη	i briyandini
wavy	κυματιστά	kimatista

AT THE HAIRDRESSER

I'd like to make an appointment
Θα ήθελα να κλείσω ένα ραντεβού
THA iTHela na kliso ena randevoo

Just a trim, please
Πάρτε τα μου λίγο, παρακαλώ
parteta moo ligo, parakalo

Not too much off
Μην κόψετε πολλά
mi kopsete pola

A bit more off here, please
Λίγο πιό πολύ εδώ, παρακαλώ
ligo pio poli etho, parakalo

I'd like a cut and blow-dry
Θα ήθελα ένα κούρεμα και χτένισμα
THA iTHela ena koorema ke htenisma

I'd like a perm
Θα ήθελα μία περμανάντ
THA iTHela mia permanant

I'd like highlights
Θα ήθελα να κάνω μες
THA iTHela'na kano mes

THINGS YOU'LL SEE

ανδρικές κομμώσεις	*anthrikes komosis*	men's hairdresser
βαφή	*vafi*	hair dye
βάφω	*vafo*	to tint
ίσια	*isia*	straight
γυναικείες κομμώσεις	*yinekies komosis*	women's salon
κόβω	*kovo*	to cut
κομμώσεις	*komosis*	hairstylist
κομμώτρια	*komotria*	hairdresser
κουρέας	*kooreas*	barber
κουρείο	*koorio*	barber (shop)
κούρεμα	*koorema*	haircut
λούσιμο	*loosimo*	wash
μαλλιά	*malia*	hair
μες	*mes*	highlights
μιζανπλί	*mizanpli*	set
ξύρισμα	*xirisma*	shave
περμανάντ	*permanant*	perm
ρολά	*rola*	curlers
σαμπουάν	*sampooan*	shampoo
σγουρά	*sgoora*	curly
στεγνώνω	*stegnono*	to dry
τα μπροστινά	*ta brostina*	the front
τα πλαϊνά	*ta plaina*	on the sides
τα πίσω	*ta piso*	at the back

SPORT

Thanks to Greece's excellent climate, almost all outdoor sports are well catered for. Along the coasts of the mainland and on the islands there are excellent opportunities for swimming, water-skiing, sailing, fishing (including underwater fishing), canoeing and sailboarding. You will easily find someone to teach you water-skiing or windsurfing, and hiring equipment generally poses no problem, with everything from a parasol to a sailboard being available at a reasonable charge.

If you want to discover the rarer beauties of Greece and the Archipelago, then you must take to the sea. There are beautiful beaches, small islands and sea caves accessible only by water. If you don't want to sail solo, there are several companies who will provide you with a captain – and a crew as well if you like. Detailed information is available from the Yacht Club of Greece. In the mountainous areas such as the Pindos range, Parnassos (near Delphi), Parnitha (just north of Athens), or Olympus, there is ample scope for walking and mountaineering. In the winter there is even skiing.

USEFUL WORDS AND PHRASES

athletics	ο αθλητισμός	o aτHlitismos
ball	η μπάλα	i bala
beach	η παραλία	i paralia
bicycle	το ποδήλατο	to pothilato
canoe	το κανώ	to kano
deck chair	η πολυθρόνα	i poliτHrona
diving board	η σανίδα	i sanitha
fishing	το ψάρεμα	to psarema
fishing rod	το καλάμι	to kalami
flippers	τα βατραχοπέδιλα	ta vatrahopethila
football	το ποδόσφαιρο	to pothosfero
football match	ο ποδοσφαιρικός αγώνας	o pothosferikos agonas

goggles	η μάσκα	i maska
golf	το γκολφ	to 'golf'
golf course	το γήπεδο του γκολφ	to yipetho too 'golf'
gymnastics	η γυμναστική	i yimnastiki
harpoon	το ψαροντούφεκο	to psarodoofeko
jogging	το τζόγκινγκ	to 'jogging'
lake	η λίμνη	i limni
mountaineering	η ορειβασία	i orivasia
oxygen bottles	οι μπουκάλες οξυγόνου	i bookales oxigonoo
pedal boat	το ποδήλατο θαλάσσης	to pothilato THalasis
racket	η ρακέτα	i raketa
riding	η ιππασία	i ipasia
rowing boat	η βάρκα με κουπιά	i varka me koopia
run (verb)	τρέχω	treho
sailboard	το γουίντ-σέρφινγκ	to 'windsurfing'
sailing	η ιστιοπλοΐα	i istioplo-ia
sand	η άμμος	i amos
sea	η θάλασσα	i THalasa
skin diving	οι υποβρύχιες καταδύσεις	i ipovri-hies katathisis
snorkel	ο αναπνευστήρας	o anapnefstiras
stadium	το στάδιο	to stathio
sunshade	η ομπρέλα του ήλιου	i obrela too ilioo
swim (verb)	κολυμπώ	kolibo
swimming pool	η πισίνα	i pisina
tennis	το τέννις	to 'tennis'
tennis court	το γήπεδο του τέννις	to yipetho too 'tennis'
tennis racket	η ρακέτα	i raketa
tent	η σκηνή	i skini
underwater fishing	το υποβρύχιο ψάρεμα	to ipovrihio psarema

volleyball	το βόλλεϋ	to 'volley'
walking	το περπάτημα	to perpatima
water-skiing	το θαλάσσιο σκι	to THalasio 'ski'
water-skis	τα πέδιλα του σκι	ta pethila too 'ski'
wave	το κύμα	to kima
wet suit	η στολή	i stoli
	βατραχανθρώπου	vatrahanTHropou
yacht	το γιώτ	to 'yacht'

How do I get to the beach?
Πως μπορώ να πάω στην παραλία;
pos boro na pao stin paralia

How deep is the water here?
Πόσο βαθύ είναι το νερό εδώ;
poso vaTHi ine to nero etho

Is there a swimming pool here?
Υπάρχει καμμία πισίνα εδώ;
iparhi kamia pisina etho

Is it safe to swim here?
Είναι ασφαλές το κολύμπι εδώ;
ine asfales to kolimbi etho

Can I fish here?
Μπορώ να ψαρέψω εδώ;
boro na psarepso etho

Do I need a licence?
Χρειάζομαι δίπλωμα;
hriazome thiploma

How much does it cost per hour/day?
Πόσο στοιχίζει την ώρα/ημέρα;
poso sti-hizi tin ora/imera

Am I allowed to camp here?
Επιτρέπεται να κατασκηνώσω εδώ;
epitrepete na kataskinoso etho

I would like to take water-skiing lessons
Θα ήθελα να πάρω μαθήματα σκι
THa itHela na paro matHimata 'ski'

Where can I hire …?
Που μπορώ να νοικιάσω …;
poo boro na nikiaso

THINGS YOU'LL SEE OR HEAR

αθλητικές εγκαταστάσεις	*aTHlitikes egatastasis*	sporting facilities
αθλητικό κέντρο	*aTHlitiko kendro*	sports centre
ακτή	*akti*	beach
άλσος	*alsos*	wooded park
απαγορεύεται η κατασκήνωση	*apagorevete i kataskinosi*	no camping
απαγορεύεται η κολύμβηση	*apagorevete i kolimvisi*	no swimming
απαγορεύεται το ψάρεμα	*apagorevete to psarema*	no fishing
απαγορευμένη περιοχή	*apagorevmeni periohi*	restricted area
απαγορεύονται οι καταδύσεις	*apagorevonde i katathisis*	no diving
γήπεδο	*yipetho*	football pitch
γήπεδο τέννις	*yipetho 'tennis'*	tennis court
εισιτήρια	*isitiria*	tickets
ενοικιάζονται	*enikiazonde*	for hire
θαλάσσια σπορ	*THalasia spor*	water sports

→

ππόδρομος	*ipothromos*	racecourse (for horses)
ιστιοφόρο	*istioforo*	sailing boat
κωπηλατώ	*kopilato*	to row
λιμενική Αστυνομία	*limeniki astinomia*	harbour police
λιμήν	*limin*	port
μαρίνα	*marina*	marina
μαθήματα σκι	*maTHimata 'ski'*	water-skiing lessons
πρώτες βοήθειες	*protes voiTHies*	first aid
ποδήλατα	*pothilata*	bicycles
στάδιο	*stathio*	stadium
χώρος διά ποδηλάτες	*horos ia pothilates*	cycle path

POST OFFICES AND BANKS

Post offices in Greece only deal with mail, so don't expect to find telephones there. (If you want to make a phone call, use a call box or go to the telephone exchange – OTE). Stamps can be bought in post offices but many Greeks go to street kiosks where you can also buy your postcards. Letter boxes are usually bright yellow. Mail can be sent to you, marked poste restante, for collection at the post office of any town. You will need to show your passport as indentification when you pick up any mail. Post offices are generally open from 7.30 am to 2 pm Monday to Friday, with some main branches staying open as late as 8 pm. Some main post offices also open for a few hours at weekends.

All banks are open from 8 am to 2 pm Monday to Thursday, and 8 am to 1.30 pm on Friday. In larger towns and resorts, at least one bank will reopen briefly for currency exchange in the evening and on Saturday mornings during the summer season. Banks close for public holidays and sometimes for local festivals. Cash machines are found in major towns and resorts, but seldom elsewhere.

The Greek unit of currency is the common European currency, the euro (**ευρώ** evro). One euro is divided into 100 cents (**λεπτό** lepto). The coins come in 1, 2, 5, 10, 20 and 50 cents; 1 and 2 euros. Notes are available in 5, 10, 20, 50, 100, 200 and 500 euros.

The best exchange rates for currency, traveller's cheques and Eurocheques are found in banks and post offices, although you can also change money in travel agencies, hotels, tourist offices and car hire agencies. Some large towns also have electronic currency exchange machines.

Credit cards are not generally accepted at inexpensive restaurants and shops, but they are useful in most hotels and for large purchases. They can also be used to obtain cash advances in some banks and from cash machines. There may be a processing charge for such transactions.

Useful Words and Phrases

airmail	αεροπορικώς	*aeroporikos*
bank	η τράπεζα	*i trapeza*
banknote	το χαρτονόμισμα	*to hartonomisma*
cash	τα μετρητά	*ta metrita*
cash machine	το μηχάνημα ανάληψης μετρητών	*to mihanima analipsis metriton*
change (*noun*)	το συνάλλαγμα	*to sinalagma*
(*verb*)	αλλάζω συνάλλαγμα	*allazo sinalagma*
cheque	η επιταγή	*i epitayi*
chequebook	το βιβλιάριο επιταγών	*to vivliario epitagon*
coins	κέρματα	*kermata*
counter	το ταμείο	*to tamio*
credit card	η πιστωτική κάρτα	*i pistotiki karta*
customs form	τελωνιακή δήλωση	*teloniaki thilosi*
delivery	η διανομή	*i thianomi*
deposit (*noun*)	η κατάθεση	*kataTHesi*
(*verb*)	καταθέτω	*kataTHeto*
exchange rate	η συναλλαγματική ισοτιμία	*i sinalagmatiki isotimia*
form	η αίτηση	*i etisi*
international money order	η διεθνής τραπεζική εντολή πληρωμής	*i thieTHnis trapeziki endoli pliromis*
letter	το γράμμα	*to grama*
letter box	το γραμματοκιβώτιο	*to gramatokivotio*
mail	το ταχυδρομείο	*to tahithromio*
money order	η ταχυδρομική επιταγή	*i tahithromiki epitayi*
package/parcel	το δέμα	*to thema*
post	το ταχυδρομείο	*to tahithromio*
postage rates	τα ταχυδρομικά έξοδα	*ta tahithromika exotha*

postal order	η ταχυδρομική επιταγή	i tahithromik̲i̲ epitay̲i̲
postcard	η κάρτα	i k̲a̲rta
postcode	ο ταχυδρομικός τομέας	o tahithromik̲o̲s tom̲e̲as
poste restante	το ποστ-ρεστάντ	to post-rest̲a̲nt
postman	ο ταχυδρόμος	o tahithr̲o̲mos
post office	το ταχυδρομείο	to tahithrom̲i̲o
pound sterling	η λίρα στερλίνα	l̲i̲ra sterl̲i̲na
registered letter	το συστημένο γράμμα	to sistim̲e̲no gr̲a̲ma
stamp	το γραμματόσημο	to gramat̲o̲simo
traveller's cheque	η ταξιδιωτική επιταγή	i taxithiotik̲i̲ epitay̲i̲
US dollar	το Αμερικανικό δολλάριο	amerikanik̲o̲ thol̲a̲rio
withdraw	κάνω ανάληψη	k̲a̲no an̲a̲lipsi
withdrawal	η ανάληψη	i an̲a̲lipsi

How much is a letter/postcard to …?
Πόσο κάνει το γραμματόσημο για ένα γράμμα/μία κάρτα για …;
p̲o̲so k̲a̲ni to gramat̲o̲simo ya ̲e̲na gr̲a̲ma/m̲i̲a k̲a̲rta ya

I would like three 50 cent stamps
Θα ήθελα τρία γραμματόσημα των πενήντα λεπτών
THa ̲i̲THela tr̲i̲a gramat̲o̲sima ton pen̲i̲nda lept̲o̲n

I want to register this letter
Θέλω να στείλω αυτό το γράμμα συστημένο
THe̲lo na st̲i̲lo aft̲o̲ to gr̲a̲ma sistim̲e̲no

I want to send this parcel to …
Θέλω να στείλω αυτό το δέμα στην …
THe̲lo na st̲i̲lo aft̲o̲ to th̲e̲ma stin

How long does the post to … take?
Πόσο κάνει να φτάσει στην …;
poso kani na ftasi stin

Where can I post this?
Που μπορώ να ταχυδρομήσω αυτό;
poo boro na tahithromiso afto

Is there any mail for me?
Υπάρχει κανένα γράμμα για μένα;
iparhi kanena grama ya mena?

This is to go airmail
Αυτό να πάει αεροπορικώς
afto na pai aeroporikos

I'd like to change this into 20 euro notes
Θα ήθελα να το αλλάξω αυτό σε χαρτονομίσματα των
  είκοσι ευρώ
THa itHela na to alaxo afto se hartonomismata ton ikosi evro

Can I cash these traveller's cheques?
Μπορώ να εξαργυρώσω αυτές τις ταξιδιωτικές επιταγές;
boro na exargyroso aftes tis taxithiotikes epitayes

What is the exchange rate for the pound?
Ποιά είναι η τιμή συναλλάγματος για τη στερλίνα;
pia ine i timi sinalagmatos yia ti sterlina

Can I draw cash using this credit card?
Μπορώ να πάρω μετρητά με αυτή την πιστωτική κάρτα;
boro na paro metrita me afti tin pistotiki karta

Could you give me smaller notes?
Μπορείτε να μου δώσετε μικρότερα χαρτονομίσματα;
borite na moo thosete mikrotera hartonomismata

THINGS YOU'LL SEE

αεροπορικώς	*aeroporikos*	by air mail
αλλαγή	*allayi*	currency
συναλλάγματος	*sinalagmatos*	exchange
αναλήψεις	*analipsis*	withdrawals
ανοικτά	*anikta*	open
αποστολέας	*apostoleas*	sender
γραμματοκιβώτιο	*gramatokivotio*	letter box
γραμματόσημο	*gramatosima*	stamps
δέματα	*themata*	parcels, packages
διεύθυνση	*thi-efthinsi*	address
ΕΛΤΑ	*elta*	Greek Post Office
εξωτερικού	*exoterikoo*	postage abroad
επιστολές	*epistoles*	letters
εσωτερικό	*esoterikoo*	inland postage
καρτ-ποστάλ	*kart-postal*	postcard
καταθέσεις	*kataτHesis*	deposits
κατεπείγον	*katepigon*	express
κλειστά	*klista*	closed
μηχάνημα ανάληψης	*mihanima analipsis*	cash machine
μετρητών	*metriton*	
ξένο νόμισμα	*xeno nomisma*	foreign currency
ποστ-ρεστάντ	*post restant*	poste restante
συνάλλαγμα	*sinalagma*	exchange
συστημένα	*sistimena*	registered mail
ταμείο	*tamio*	cash desk
ταμίας	*tamias*	cashier
ταχυδρομείο	*tahithromio*	post office
ταχυδρομικός	*tahithromikos*	postcode
τομεύς	*tomefs*	
τηλεγραφήμματα	*tilegrafimata*	telegrams
τιμές	*times*	exchange rates
συναλλάγματος	*sinalagmatos*	
τράπεζα	*trapeza*	bank

→

τραπεζικές εντολές πληρωμής	*trapezikes endoles pliromis*	money orders
τρέχοντες λογαριασμοί	*trehondes logariasmi*	current accounts
φάξ	*fax*	fax (machine)
φωτοτυπικό μηχάνημα	*fototipiko mihanima*	photocopier
ώρες λειτουργίας	*ores litooryias*	opening hours

COMMUNICATIONS

Telephones: Telephones are the responsibility of the OTE (Telecommunications Organisation of Greece) not of the post office. Don't forget that the little Greek kiosks where you can buy cigarettes, postcards etc, also have a telephone for public use. There are also payphones in cafeterias and restaurants. If you want to make a call home, or a long-distance call within Greece, you can either use a phonecard or go to an OTE office. There, you will be given a booth and asked to pay at the desk when you have finished your call.

The tones you'll hear when making a call in Greece are:

Dialling tone:	same as in UK
Ringing:	repeated long tone
Engaged:	rapid pips

Dialling codes: UK 0044; USA 001

Useful telephone numbers:

Ambulance	165
Police	100
Tourist Police	171
Fire	199
Roadside assistance	174

USEFUL WORDS AND PHRASES

call	το τηλεφώνημα	to tilefonima
to call	τηλεφωνώ	tilefono
code	ο κωδικός	o kothikos
crossed line	η μπλεγμένη γραμμή	i blegmeni grami
to dial	καλώ	kalo
emergency	η επείγουσα ανάγκη	i epigoosa anagi
enquiries	οι πληροφορίες	i plirofories

extension	το εσωτερικό	to esoteriko
international call	το υπεραστικό	to iperastiko
mobile phone	το κινητό τηλέφωνο	tokinito tilefono
number	ο αριθμός	o ariTHmos
payphone	το τηλέφωνο με κέρματα	to tilefono me kermata
phonecard	η τηλεφωνική κάρτα	i tilefoniki karta,
receiver	το ακουστικό	to akoostiko
reverse charge call	το τηλεφώνημα κολέκτ	to tilefonima kolekt
telephone	το τηλέφωνο	to tilefono
telephone box	ο τηλεφωνικός θάλαμος	o tilefonikos THalamos
telephone directory	ο τηλεφωνικός κατάλογος	o tilefonikos katalogos
wrong number	λάθος νούμερο	laTHos noomero

Where is the nearest phone box?
Που είναι ο πλησιέστερος τηλεφωνικός θάλαμος;
poo ine o plisi-esteros tilefonikos THalamos

Hello, this is … speaking
Χαίρετε, είμαι ο/η …
herete, ime o/i

Is that …?
Ο/η …;
o/i

Speaking
ο ίδιος
o ithios

I would like to speak to …
Θα ήθελα να μιλήσω στον …
THa iTHela na miliso ston

Extension ..., please
Εσωτερικό ... παρακαλώ
esoteriko ... parakalo

Please tell him ... called
Παρακαλώ του λέτε ότι τηλεφώνησε ο/η ...
parakalo too lete oti tilefonise o/i

Ask him to call me back, please
Πέστε του να με ξαναπάρει παρακαλώ
peste too na me xanapari parakalo

My number is ...
το τηλέφωνό μου είναι ...
to tilefono moo ine

Do you know where he is?
Ξέρετε που είναι;
xerete poo ine

When will he be back?
Πότε θα επιστρέψει;
pote tha epistrepsi

Could you leave him a message?
Μπορείτε να του αφήσετε ένα μήνυμα;
borite na too afisete ena minimas

I'll ring back later
Θα σε ξαναπάρω αργότερα
tha se xanaparo argotera

Sorry, wrong number
Πήρατε λάθος αριθμό
pirate lathos arithmo

Is there a telephone directory?
Υπάρχει κανένας τηλεφωνικός κατάλογος;
iparhi kanenas tilefonikos katalogos

I would like the directory for …
Θα ήθελα τον κατάλογο για …
THa iTHela ton katalogo ya

Can I call abroad from here?
Μπορώ να τηλεφωνήσω στο εξωτερικό από εδώ;
boro na tilefoniso sto exoteriko apo etho

How much is a call to …?
Πόσο στοιχίζει ένα τηλεφώνημα στο …;
poso sti-hizi ena tilefonima sto

I would like to reverse the charges
Θα ήθελα τα έξοδα να πληρωθούν εκεί
THa iTHela ta exotha na pliroTHoon eki

I would like a number in …
Θέλω ένα αριθμό στην …
THelo ena ariTHmo stin

What's your fax number/What's your email address?
Ποιός είναι ο αριθμός του φαξ/Ποιά είναι η διεύθυνση (email);
pios ine o arithmos too fax/pia ine i thiefTHinsi 'email'

Did you get my fax/email?
Έλαβες το φαξ/email μου;
elaves to fax/'email'

Please resend your fax
Παρακαλώ ξαναστείλτε το φαξ
parakalo xanastilte to fax

Can I send a fax/email from here?
Μπορώ να στείλω φαξ/email από εδώ;
boro na stilo fax/'email' apo etho

Can I use the photocopier/fax machine?
Μπορώ νά χρησιμοποιήσω το φωτοτυπικό μηχάνημα/το φαξ;
boro na hrisimopiiso tin fototipiko mihanima/to fax

How do I get an outside line?
Πως παίρνω εξωτερική γραμμή;
pos perno exoteriki grami

THINGS YOU'LL SEE OR HEAR

ακουστικό	*akoostiko*	receiver
άμεσος δράσις	*amesos thrasis*	emergencies, police
αριθμός	*ariTHmos*	number
δεν λειτουργεί	*then litooryi*	out of order
καλεί	*kali*	ringing
καλέσατε	*kalesate*	dial
κέρματα	*kermata*	coins
κωδικός	*kothikos*	code
λάθος νούμερο	*laTHos noomero*	wrong number
μιλάει	*milai*	engaged
μονάδες	*monathes*	units
νούμερο	*noomero*	number
πυροσβεστική	*pirosvestiki*	fire brigade
σηκώσατε	*sikosate*	pick up
τηλεφώνημα	*tilefonima*	call
τηλεφωνώ	*tilefono*	to call
τοπικό	*topiko*	local call
χαίρετε	*herete*	Hello
χρυσός οδηγός	*hrisos othigos*	Yellow Pages
υπεραστικό	*iperastiko*	long-distance call, international call

THINGS YOU'LL HEAR

O ithios
Speaking

Lipame, then ine etho
Sorry, he's not in

Pios tilefoni?
Who's calling?

Me pion THelete na milisete?
Who would you like to speak to?

Bori na sas pari piso?
Can he call you back?

Pio ine to tilefono sas?
What's your number?

Pirate lathos noomero
You've got the wrong number

THa epistrepsi stis …
He'll be back at …

THa sas sintheso
I'll put you through

HEALTH

Under EC Social Security regulations visitors from the UK qualify for treatment on the same basis as Greeks themselves. You must complete an E111 form (available from Post offices) before you travel.

If you fall ill or have an accident – nothing too serious – you can always go to a pharmacist, who is usually qualified to treat minor injuries. Chemists' (*to farmakio*) are identified by a red or green cross, and all towns have one that is open all night on a rota system: look for a sign on the door telling you which is the duty chemist.

USEFUL WORDS AND PHRASES

accident	το ατύχημα	*to atihima*
ambulance	το ασθενοφόρο	*to asthenoforo*
anaemic	αναιμικός	*anemikos*
appendicitis	η σκωληκοειδίτις	*i skoliko-ithitis*
appendix	η σκωληκοειδής απόφυση	*i skoliko-ithis apofisi*
aspirin	η ασπιρίνη	*i aspirini*
asthma	το άσθμα	*to asthma*
backache	ο πόνος στη πλάτη	*o ponos sti plati*
bandage	ο επίδεσμος	*o epithesmos*
bite	το δάγκωμα	*to thagoma*
(by insect)	το τσίμπημα	*to tssbima*
bladder	η κύστη	*i kisti*
blister	η φουσκάλα	*i fooskala*
blood	το αίμα	*to ema*
blood donor	ο αιμοδότης	*o emothotis*
burn	το κάψιμο	*o kapsimo*
cancer	ο καρκίνος	*o karkinos*
chemist	ο φαρμακοποιός	*o farmakopios*
chest	το στήθος	*to stithos*
chickenpox	η ανεμοβλογιά	*i anemovloya*

cold	το κρυολόγημα	*to krioloyima*
concussion	η διάσειση	*i thiasisi*
constipation	η δυσκοιλιότητα	*i thiskiliotita*
contact lenses	οι φακοί επαφής	*i faki epafis*
corn	ο κάλος	*o kalos*
cough	ο βήχας	*o vihas*
cut	το κόψιμο	*to kopsimo*
dentist	ο οδοντίατρος	*o othondiatros*
diabetes	το ζάχαρο	*to zaharo*
diarrhoea	η διάρροια	*i thiaria*
dizzy	ζαλισμένος	*zalismenos*
doctor	ο γιατρός	*o yatros*
earache	ο πόνος στ᾽αυτί	*o ponos st'afti*
fever	ο πυρετός	*o piretos*
filling	το σφράγισμα	*to sfrayisma*
first aid	οι πρώτες βοήθειες	*i protes voiтHies*
flu	η γρίππη	*i gripi*
fracture	το κάταγμα	*to katagma*
German measles	η ερυθρά	*i eriтHra*
glasses	τα γυαλιά	*ta yalia*
haemorrhage	η αιμοραγία	*i emorayia*
hay fever	ο πυρετός	*o piretos*
	του χόρτου	*too hortoo*
headache	ο πονοκέφαλος	*o ponokefalos*
heart	η καρδιά	*i karthia*
heart attack	η καρδιακή	*i karthiaki*
	προσβολή	*prosvoli*
hospital	το νοσοκομείο	*to nosokomio*
ill	άρρωστος	*arostos*
indigestion	η δυσπεψία	*i thispepsia*
injection	η ένεση	*i enesi*
itch	η φαγούρα	*i fagoura*
kidney	το νεφρό	*to nefro*
lump	ο όγκος	*o ogos*
measles	η ιλαρά	*i ilara*
migraine	η ημικρανία	*i imikrania*

mumps	οι μαγουλάδες	i magoolathes
nausea	η ναυτία	i naftia
nurse	η νοσοκόμα	i nosokoma
operation	η εγχείρηση	i enhirisi
optician	ο οπτικός	o optikos
pain	ο πόνος	o ponos
penicillin	η πενικιλλίνη	i penikilini
plaster	ο γύψος	o yipsos
pneumonia	η πνευμονία	i pnevmonia
pregnant	έγκυος	egios
prescription	η συνταγή	i sindayi
rheumatism	οι ρευματισμοί	i revmatismi
scald	το έγκαυμα	to egavma
scratch	η γρατζουνιά	i grazoonia
smallpox	η ευλογιά	i evloya
splinter	η αγκίδα	i agitha
sprain	το διάστρεμμα	to thiastrema
sting	το τσούξιμο	to tsooximo
stomach	το στομάχι	to stomahi
temperature	ο πυρετός	o piretos
tonsils	οι αμυγδαλές	i amigthales
toothache	ο πονόδοντος	o ponothondos
travel sickness	η ναυτία	i naftia
ulcer	το έλκος	to elkos
vaccination	ο εμβολιασμός	o emvoliasmos
vomit (verb)	κάνω εμετό	kano emeto
whooping cough	ο κοκκύτης	o kokitis

I have a pain in …
Έχω ένα πόνο στο …
eho ena pono sto

I do not feel well
Δεν αισθάνομαι καλά
then esthanome kala

I feel faint
Μου έρχετε λιποθυμία
moo erhete lipoτHimia

I feel sick
Θα κάνω εμετό
THa kano emeto

I feel dizzy
Ζαλίζομαι
zalizome

I have a sore throat
Πονάει ο λαιμός μου
ponai o lemos moo

It hurts here
Πονάει εδώ
ponai etho

It's a sharp pain
Είναι δυνατός πόνος
ine thinatos ponos

It's a dull pain
Έχω ένα μικρό πόνο
eho ena mikro pono

It hurts all the time
Πονάει συνέχεια
ponai sinehia

It only hurts now and then
Με πονάει πότε-πότε
me ponai pote-pote

It hurts when you touch it
Με πονάει όταν το ακουμπάς
me ponai otan to akoobas

It hurts more at night
Πονάει περισσότερο την νύχτα
ponai perisotero ti nihta

It stings/It aches
Τσούζει/Πονάει
tsoozi/ponai

I have a temperature
Έχω πυρετό
eho pireto

I'm ... months pregnant
Είμαι ... μηνών έγκυος
ime ...minon egios

I need a prescription for ...
Χρειάζομαι συνταγή για ...
hriazome sidayi ya

I normally take ...
Συνήθως παίρνω ...
siniTHos perno

I'm allergic to ...
Είμαι αλλεργικός με ...
ime aleryikos me

Have you got anything for ...?
Εχετε τίποτα για ...;
ehete tipota ya

Can you take these if you are pregnant/breastfeeding?
Μπορείς να τα πάρεις εάν είσαι έγκυος/θηλάζεις;
boris na ta paris ean ise egios/thilazis

Do I need a prescription for …?
Χρειάζομαι συνταγή για …;
hriazome sindayi ya

I have lost a filling
Μου έφυγε ένα σφράγισμα
moo efiye ena sfrayisma

THINGS YOU'LL SEE

αίθουσα αναμονής	*eTHoosa anamonis*	waiting room
ακτίνες-Χ	*aktines hi*	X-rays
ασθενοφόρο	*asTHenoforo*	ambulance
αφροδισιολόγος	*afrothisiologos*	venereal specialist
γιατρός	*yatros*	doctor
γυαλιά	*yalia*	glasses
γυναικολόγος	*yinekologos*	gynaecologist
δερματολόγος	*thermatologos*	dermatologist
διανυκτερεύον	*thianikterevon*	open all night
ειδικός	*ithikos*	specialist
εξετάσεις	*exetasis*	check-up
ησυχία	*isihia*	quiet
ιατρείο	*iatrio*	doctor's surgery
ιατρός	*iatros*	doctor
κλινική	*kliniki*	clinic
νοσοκόμα	*nosokoma*	nurse
νοσοκομείο	*nosokomio*	hospital
οδοντίατρος	*othondiatros*	dentist
οδοντιατρείο	*othondiatrio*	dentist's
ούλο	*oolo*	gum
οπτικός	*optikos*	optician

παθολόγος	paTHologos	GP
παιδίατρος	pethiatros	paediatrician
πίεση αίματος	pi-esi ematos	blood pressure
πρώτες βοήθειες	protes voiTHi-es	first aid
σφράγισμα	sfrayisma	filling
τοπική αναισθησία	topiki anesTHisia	local anesthetic
φαρμακείο	farmakio	chemist (shop)
φαρμακοποιός	farmakopios	chemist
χειρουργείο	hirooryio	operating theatre
ώρες επισκέψεως	ores episkepseos	visiting hours

THINGS YOU'LL HEAR

Na pernis … hapia tin imera
Take … pills/tablets per day

Me nero
With water

Na ta masate
Chew them

Mia fora/thio fores/tris fores tin imera
Once/twice/three times a day

Mono otan pas ya ipno
Only when you go to bed

Ti pernis siniTHos?
What do you normally take?

Prepi na this ena yatro
I think you should see a doctor

Lipame, then to ehoome
I'm sorry, we don't have that

Hriazese sindayi yafto
For that you need a prescription

CONVERSION TABLES

DISTANCES

Distances are marked in kilometres. To convert kilometres to miles, divide the km by 8 and multiply by 5 (1 km being five-eighths of a mile). Convert miles to km by dividing the miles by 5 and multiplying by 8. A mile is 1609 m (1.609 km).

km	miles or km	miles
1.61	1	0.62
3.22	2	1.24
4.83	3	1.86
6.44	4	2.48
8.05	5	3.11
9.66	6	3.73
11.27	7	4.35
12.88	8	4.97
14.49	9	5.59
16.10	10	6.21

Other units of length:

1 centimetre	= 0.39 in	1 inch = 25.4 millimetres
1 metre	= 39.37 in	1 foot = 0.30 metre (30 cm)
10 metres	= 32.81 ft	1 yard = 0.91 metre

WEIGHTS

The unit you will come into most contact with is the kilogram (kilo), equivalent to 2 lb 3oz. To convert kg to lbs, multiply by 2 and add one-tenth of the result (thus, 6 kg x 2 = 12 + 1.2, or 13.2 lbs). One ounce is about 28 grams, and 1 lb is 454 g.

grams	ounces	ounces	grams
50	1.76	1	28.3
100	3.53	2	56.7
250	8.81	4	113.4
500	17.63	8	226.8

kg	lbs or kg	lbs
0.45	1	2.20
0.91	2	4.41
1.36	3	6.61
1.81	4	8.82
2.27	5	11.02
2.72	6	13.23
3.17	7	15.43
3.63	8	17.64
4.08	9	19.84
4.53	10	22.04

TEMPERATURE

To convert centigrade or Celsius degrees into Fahrenheit, the accurate method is to multiply the °C figure by 1.8 and add 32. Similarly, to convert °F to °C, subtract 32 from the °F figure and divide by 1.8. This will give you a truly accurate conversion, but it takes a little time in mental arithmetic! See the table below:

°C	°F	°C	°F	
-10	14	25	77	
0	32	30	86	
5	41	36.9	98.4	*body temperature*
10	50	40	104	
20	68	100	212	*boiling point*

LIQUIDS

Drivers from the UK will be used to seeing petrol priced per litre (and may even know that one litre is about 1.75 pints). One 'imperial' gallon is roughly 4.5 litres, but American drivers must remember that the US gallon is only 3.8 litres (1 litre = 1.06 US quart). In the following table, imperial gallons are used:

litres	gals _or_ l	gals
4.54	1	0.22
9.10	2	0.44
13.64	3	0.66
18.18	4	0.88
22.73	5	1.10
27.27	6	1.32
31.82	7	1.54
36.37	8	1.76
40.91	9	1.98
45.46	10	2.20
90.92	20	4.40
136.38	30	6.60
181.84	40	8.80
227.30	50	11.00

TYRE PRESSURES

lb/sq in	15	18	20	22	24
kg/sq cm	1.1	1.3	1.4	1.5	1.7

lb/sq in	26	28	30	33	35
kg/sq cm	1.8	2.0	2.1	2.3	2.5

MINI-DICTIONARY

about: about 16 peripoo thekaexi
accelerator to gazi
accident to thistihima
accommodation thomatia
ache o ponos
adaptor *(electrical)* to polaplo
address i thiefтнinsi
adhesive i kola
admission charge i isothos
after meta
aftershave i kolonia meta to
   xirisma
again xana
against enandion
air conditioning o klimatismos
aircraft to aeroplano
air freshener to aposmitiko horoo
air hostess i aerosinothos
airline i aerogrami
airport to aerothromio
Albania i Alvania
Albanian *(man)* o Alvanos
   (woman) i Alvani
   (adj) Alvanikos
alcohol to alko-ol
all ola
   all the streets oli i thromi
   that's all, thanks tipota alo,efharisto
almost s-hethon
alone monos
already ithi
always panda
am: I am ime
ambulance to asтненoforo
America i Ameriki
American *(man)* o Amerikanos
   (woman) i Amerikana
   (adj) Amerikanikos

and ke
ankle o astragalos
anorak to boofan
another *(room)* alo
   (coffee) kialo
answering machine o aftomatos tilefonitis
antifreeze to andipsiktiko
antique shop to paleopolio
antiseptic to andisiptiko
apartment to thiamerisma
appendicitis i skolikoithitis
appetite i orexi
apple to milo
application form i etisi
appointment to radevoo
apricot to verikoko
are: you are ise
   we are imaste
   they are ine
arm to heri
art i tehni
art gallery i pinakoтнiki
artist o kalitehnis
as: as soon as possible oso pio
   grigora yinete
ashtray to stahtothohio
asleep: he's asleep kimate
aspirin i aspirini
at: at the post office sto tahithromio
   at night ti nihta
   at 3 o'clock stis tris i ora
Athens i Aтнina
attractive elkistikos
aunt i thia
Australia i Afstralia
Australian *(man)* o Afstralos
   (woman) i Afstraleza
   (adj) Afstralezikos

Austria i Afstrịa
Austrian (man) o Afstriakọs
   (woman) i Afstriakị
   (adj) Afstriakọs
automatic aftọmatos
away: is it far away? ịne makrịa?
   go away! fịye!
awful apẹsios
axe to tsekọori
axle o ạxonas

baby to morọ
baby wipes igrạ hartomạnthila
back (not front) pịso
   (body) i platị
bacon to beikon
   bacon and eggs avgạ me beikon
bad kakọs
bait to thọloma
bake psịno
baker o fọornaris
balcony to balkọni
ball (football) i balạ
   (tennis) to balạki
   (dance) i horosperịtha
ballpoint pen o markathọros
banana i bananạ
band (musicians) to sigrọtima
bandage o epịthesmos
bank i trạpeza
banknote to hartonọmisma
bar to bar
   bar of chocolate i sokolạta
barbecue to psịsimo stin exohị
barber's to koorịo
bargain i efkerịa
basement to ipọyio
basin (sink) o niptịras
basket to kalạTHi
bath to banịo
   to have a bath kạno banịo
bathing hat o skọofos too banịoo

bathroom to banịo
battery i batarịa
beach i paralịa
beans ta fasọlia
beard ta yenịa
because epithị
bed to krevạti
bed linen ta sendọnia
bedroom to ipnothomạtio
beef to mos-harị
beer i bịra
before prin
beginner o arharios
behind apọ pịso
beige bez
Belgian (man) o Vẹlgos
   (woman) i Velyịtha
   (adj) Velyikọs
Belgium to Vẹlyio
bell (church) i kabạna
   (door) to koothọoni
below apọ kạto
belt i zọni
beside thịpla apọ
best ạristos
better kalịteros
between metaxị
bicycle to pothịlato
big megạlos
bikini to bikịni
bill o logariasmọs
bin liner i sakọola skoopịthion
bird to poolị
birthday ta yeneTHlịa
   happy birthday! hrọnia polạ!
birthday present to thọro ton
   yeneTHlịon
biscuit to biskọto
bite (verb) thagọno
   (noun) i thagonịa
   (by insect) to tsịbima
bitter pikrọs
black mạvros

blackberry to mooro
blanket i kooverta
bleach (*verb: hair*) xasprizo
  (*noun*) i hlorini
blind (*cannot see*) o tiflos
blister i fooskala
blood to ema
blouse i blooza
blue ble
boat to plio
  (*smaller*) to kaiki
body to soma
boil vrazo
bolt (*verb*) sirtono
  (*noun: on door*) o sirtis
bone to kokalo
bonnet (*car*) to kapo
book (*noun*) to vivlio
  (*verb*) klino
booking office
  to praktorio isitirion
bookshop to vivliopolio
boot (*car*) to port-bagaz
  (*footwear*) i bota
border ta sinora
boring varetos
born: I was born in …
  yeniтнika stin …
both ke i thio
  both of them i thio toos
  both of us i thio mas
  both … and … ke … ke …
bottle to bookali
bottle opener to anihtiri
bottom o patos
  (*sea*) o viтнos
bowl to bol
box to kooti
boy to agori
boyfriend o filos
bra to soutien
bracelet to vrahioli
braces i tirandes

brake (*noun*) to freno
  (*verb*) frenaro
brandy to koniak
bread to psomi
breakdown (*car*) i mihaniki vlavi
  (*nervous*) o nevrikos klonismos
breakfast to proino
breathe anapneo
  I can't breathe then boro na anapnefso
bridge i yefira
briefcase o hartofilakas
British Vretanikos
brochure to thiafimistiko
broken spasmeno
  broken leg to spasmeno pothi
brooch i karfitsa
brother o athelfos
brown kafes
bruise i melania
brush (*noun*) i voortsa
  (*paint*) to pinelo
  (*verb*) voortsizo
bucket o koovas
building to ktirio
Bulgaria i Voolgaria
Bulgarian (*man*) o Voolgaros
  (*woman*) i Voolgara
  (*adj*) Voolgarikos
bumper o profilahtiras
burglar o thiariktis
burn (*verb*) keo
  (*noun*) to kapsimo
bus to leoforio
bus station o staтнmos leoforion
business i thoolies
  it's none of your business
  then se afora
busy (*occupied*) katilimenos
  (*bar*) polisihnastos
but ala
butcher o hasapis
butter to vootiro
button to koobi

buy agorazo
by: by the window konda sto paraTHiro
  by Friday eos tin paraskevi
  by myself monos moo

cabbage to lahano
cable car to teleferik
cable TV i kalothiaki tileorasi
café i kafeteria
cake to 'cake'
cake shop to zaharoplastio
calculator to kompiooteraki
call: what's it called?
  pos to lene?
camera i fotografiki mihani
campsite to 'camping'
camshaft o strofalos
can (tin) i konserva
can: can I have …?
boro na eho …?
Canada o Kanathas
Canadian (man) o Kanathos
  (woman) i Kanatheza
  (adj) Kanathezikos
cancer o karkinos
candle to keri
canoe to kano
cap (bottle) to kapaki
  (hat) o skoofos
car to aftokinito
caravan to trohospito
carburettor to karbirater
card i karta
cardigan i zaketa
careful prosektikos
  be careful! prosehe!
carpet to hali
car seat (for baby/child) i pethiki karekla
aftokinitou
carriage (train) to vagoni
carrot to karoto
carrycot to port-bebe

case i valitsa
cash ta metrita
  (coins) ta psila
  to pay cash plirono metritis
cassette i kaseta
cassette player to kasetofono
castle to kastro
cat i gata
cathedral o kaTHethrikos naos
cauliflower to koonoopithi
cave i spilia
cemetery to nekrotafio
centre to kendro
certificate i athia
chair i karekla
chambermaid i kamariera
change (noun: money) ta resta
  (verb: clothes) alazo
cheap ftinos
cheers! is iyian!
cheese to tiri
chemist (shop) to farmakio
cheque i epitayi
chequebook to karne ton epitagon
cherry to kerasi
chess to skaki
chest to stiTHos
chewing gum i tsihla
chicken to kotopoolo
child to pethi
children ta pethia
china i porselani
China i Kina
Chinese (man) o Kinezos
  (woman) i Kineza
  (adj) Kinezikos
chips i tiganites patates
chocolate i sokolata
  box of chocolates to kooti me ta
  sokolatakia
chop (food) i brizola
  (to cut) kovo
church i eklisia

cigar to pooro
cigarette to tsigaro
cinema o kinimatografos
city i poli
city centre to kendro tis polis
classical music i klasiki moosiki
clean kaTHaros
clear (obvious) faneros
  (water) thiavyes
  is that clear? to katalaves?
clever exipnos
clock to roloi
  (alarm) to xipnitiri
close (near) konda
  (stuffy) apopniktikos
  (verb) klino
  the shop is closed to magazi eklise
clothes ta rooha
club to 'club'
  (cards) to bastooni
clutch to debrayaz
coach to poolman
  (of train) to vagoni
coach station o staTHmos
  iperastikon leoforion
coat to palto
coat hanger i kremastra
cockroach i katsaritha
coffee o kafes
coin to kerma
cold (adj) krios
  (illness) to krioma
collar to kolaro
collection (stamps etc) i siloyi
colour to hroma
colour film to enhromo film
comb (noun) i tsatsara
  (verb) htenizome
come erhome
  I come from ... ime apo ...
  we came last week irthame tin
  perasmeni evthomatha
  come here! ela!

communication cord to koothooni
  kinthinoo
compartment to vagoni
complicated poliplokos
concert i sinavlia
conditioner (hair) to 'conditioner'
conductor (bus) o ispraktoras
  (orchestra) o maestros
congratulations! sinharitiria!
constipation i thiskiliotis
consulate to proxenio
contact lenses i faki epafis
contraceptive to profilaktiko
cook (noun) o mayiras
  (verb) mayirevo
cooking utensils ta mayirika skevi
cool throseros
Corfu i Kerkira
cork o felos
corkscrew to anihtiri
corner i gonia
corridor o thiathromos
cosmetics ta kalindika
cost (verb) stihizo
  what does it cost? poso kani
  afto?
cotton vamvakero
cotton wool to vamvaki
cough (verb) viho
  (noun) o vihas
country (state) i hora
  (not town) i exohi
cousin (male) o exathelfos
  (female) i exathelfi
crab to kavoori
cramp i kramba
crayfish i karavitha
cream i krema
credit card i pistotiki karta
Crete i Kriti
crew to pliroma
crisps ta tsips
crowded yemato kosmo

cruise i krooaziera
crutches i pateritses
cry (weep) kleo
  (shout) fonazo
cucumber to agoori
cuff links ta maniketokooba
cup to flitzani
cupboard to doolapi
curlers ta bikooti
curls i bookles
curry metafero
curtain i koortina
Customs to Telonio
cut (noun) to kopsimo
  (verb) kovo

dad o babas
dairy (shop) to galaktopolio
damp igros
dance o horos
dangerous epikinthinos
dark skotinos
daughter i kori
day i imera
dead nekros
deaf koofos
dear (person) agapitos
  (expensive) akrivos
deck chair i politHrona
deep vatHis
deliberately epitithes
dentist o othondiatros
dentures i masela
deny arnoome
  I deny it to arnoome
deodorant to aposmitiko
department store to katastima
departure i anahorisi
develop (a film) emfanizo
diamond (jewel) to thiamandi
  (cards) to karo
diarrhoea i thiaria

diary to imeroloyio
dictionary to lexiko
die petheno
diesel to 'diesel'
different thiaforetikos
  that's different afto ine alo
  I'd like a different one THelo
  ena alo
difficult thiskolos
dining car to estiatorio too trenoo
dining room i trapezaria
directory (telephone) o tilefonikos
  katalogos
dirty vromikos
disabled anapiros
distributor (car) to distribiooter
dive vooto
diving board i sanitha
divorced horismenos
do kano
doctor o yatros
document to engrafo
dog o skilos
doll i kookla
dollar to tholario
door i porta
double room to thiplo thomatio
doughnut to donat
down kato
drawing pin i pineza
dress to forema
drink (verb) pino
  (noun) to poto
  would you like a drink?
  THelis ena poto?
drinking water to posimo nero
drive (verb) othigo
driver o othigos
driving licence to thiploma
  othiyiseos
drunk methismenos
dry stegnos
dry cleaner to stegnokatharistirio

dummy *(for baby)* i pipila
during kata ti thiarkia
dustbin o skoopithondenekes
duster to xeskonopano
Dutch Olanthikos
duty-free aforoloyita

each *(every)* kaTHenas
  twenty euros each ikosi evro to
  kaTHena
early noris
earrings ta skoolarikia
ears ta aftia
east i anatoli
easy efkolos
egg to avgo
either: either of them
  opio nane
  either ... or ... i ... i ...
elastic elastikos
elastic band to lastihaki
elbow o agonas
electric ilektrikos
electricity to ilektriko
else: something else kati alo
  someone else kapios alos
  somewhere else kapoo aloo
email to email
email address i email thiefTHinsi
embarrassing dropiastikos
embassy i presvia
embroidery to kendima
emerald to smaragthi
emergency i epigoosa anagi
empty athios
end to telos
engaged *(couple)* aravoniasmenos
  (occupied) katilimenos
engine *(motor)* i mihani
England i Anglia
English Anglikos
  (language) ta Anglika

Englishman o Anglikos
Englishwoman i Anglitha
enlargement i meyenTHisi
enough arketa
entertainment i thiaskethasi
entrance i isothos
envelope o fakelos
escalator i kinites skales
especially ithi-etera
evening to vrathi
every kaTHe
everyone oli
everything kaTHe ti
everywhere opoothipote
example to parathigma
  for example parathigmatos hari
excellent iperohos
excess baggage to ipervaro
exchange *(verb)* andalaso
exchange rate i timi sinalagmatos
excursion i ekthromi
excuse me! signomi!
exit i exothos
expensive akrivos
extension lead i proektasi
eye drops i stagones ya ta matia
eyes ta matia

face to prosopo
faint *(unclear)* asafis
  (verb) lipoTHimo
  to feel faint esTHanome lipoTHimia
fair *(funfair)* to paniyiri
  it's not fair then ine thikeo
false teeth ta pseftika thondia
family i ikoyenia
fan *(ventilator)* o anemistiras
  (enthusiast) o THavmastis
fan belt to loori too ventilater
far makria
  how far is ...?
  poso makria ine ...?

fare i timi too isitiri̱oo
farm to agroktima
farmer o agrotis
fashion i motha
fast grigoros
fat (of person) to pahos
  (on meat etc) to li̱pos
father o pateras
fax machine to fax
feel (touch) agi̱zo
  I feel hot zesteno̱me
  I feel like … eho epiTHimi̱a ya …
  I don't feel well
    then estHano̱me kala
feet ta poti̱hia
felt-tip pen o markathoros
ferry to feri-bot
fever o pi̱retos
fiancé o aravoniastikos
fiancée i aravoniastiki̱a
field o horafi̱
fig to si̱ko
filling (tooth) to sfrayisma
  (sandwich etc) i yemisi
film to 'filtro'
film to 'filtro'
filter o filtro
finger to thaktilo
fire i foti̱a
  (blaze) i pirkaya̱
fire extinguisher o pirosvesti̱ras
firework to pirote̱hnima
first protos
first aid i protes voi̱tHies
first floor to proto pato̱ma
first name to mikro onoma
fish to psari̱
fishing to psarema
  to go fishing pao ya psarema
fishing rod to psaroka̱lamo
fishmonger o psaras̱
fizzy me antHrakiko̱
flag i simea̱
flash (camera) to flas

flat (level) epi̱pethos
  (apartment) to thiame̱risma
flavour i yefsi
flea o psi̱los
flight o pti̱si
flip-flops i sayiona̱res
flippers ta vatrahope̱thila
flour to alevri̱
flower to looloo̱thi
flu i gri̱pi
flute to fla̱ooto
fly (verb) peto̱
  (insect) i mi̱ga
fog i omi̱hli
folk music i thimotiki̱ moosiki̱
food to fai̱
food poisoning i trofiki̱ thilitiri̱asi
football to potHosfero
  (ball) i bala
for ya
  for me ya mena
  what for? ya pio logo?
  for a week ya mia evthoma̱tha
foreigner o xenos
forest to thasos
fork to piro̱oni
fortnight to thekapantHi̱mero
fountain pen i pena̱
fourth tetartos
fracture to katagma
France i Gali̱a
free eleftheros
  (no cost) thore-a̱n
freezer i katapsixi
French Galikos
Frenchman o Galos
Frenchwoman i Gali̱tha
fridge to psiyi̱o
friend o fi̱los
friendly filikos
front: in front of …
  brosta̱ apo̱ …
frost i pagoni̱a

fruit to frooto
fruit juice o himos frooton
fry tiganizo
frying pan to tigani
full yematos
  I'm full hortasa
full board fool pansion
funnel (for pouring) to honi
funny astios
  (odd) peri-ergos
furniture ta epipla

garage to garaz
garden o kipos
garlic to skortho
gas-permeable lenses
  i imiskliri faki epafis
gear i tahitita
gear lever o mohlos tahititon
German (man) o Yermanos
  (woman) i Yermanitha
  (adj) Yermanikos
Germany i Yermania
get (fetch) perno
  have you got ...? ehis ...?
  to get the train
  perno to treno
get back: we get back tomorrow
  epistrefoome avrio
  to get something back
  perno kati piso
get in bes mesa
  (arrive) ftano
get out vyeno
get up (rise) sikonome
gift to thoro
gin to 'gin'
girl i kopela
girlfriend i filenatha
give thino
glad efharistimenos
  I'm glad ime eftihis

glass to yali
  (to drink) to potiri
glasses ta yalia
gloss prints i yalisteri ektiposi
gloves ta gandia
glue i kola
goggles i maska
gold o hrisos
good kalos
  good! kala!
goodbye ya hara
government i kivernisi
granddaughter i egoni
grandfather o papoos
grandmother i yaya
grandson o egonos
grapes ta stafilia
grass to grasithi
Great Britain i Megali Vretania
Greece i Elatha
Greek (man) o Elinas
  (woman) i Elinitha
  (adj) Elinikos
  (language) ta Elinika
Greek Orthodox orthothoxos
green prasinos
grey gri
grill i psistaria
grocer (shop) to bakaliko
ground floor to isoyio
ground sheet o moosamas
guarantee (noun) i egi-isi
  (verb) egioome
guard o filakas
guide book o othigos
guitar i kithara
gun (rifle) to oplo
  (pistol) to pistoli

hair ta malia
haircut (for man) to koorema
  (for woman) to kopsimo

hairdresser i komotria
hair dryer to pistolaki
hair spray i lak
half miso
  half an hour misi ora
half board i demi pansion
ham to zabon
hamburger to hamboorger
hammer to sfiri
hand to heri
handbag i tsanda
hand brake to hirofreno
handkerchief to hartomandilo
handle (door) to herooli
handsome oreos
hangover o ponokefalos
happy eftihismenos
harbour to limani
hard skliros
  (difficult) thiskolos
hard lenses i skliri faki epafis
hat to kapelo
have eho
  I don't have … then eho …
  can I have …? boro na eho …?
  have you got …? ehete …?
  I have to go now prepi na piyeno tora
hay fever o piretos ek hortoo
he aftos
head to kefali
headache o ponokefalos
headlights i provolis
hear akoo-o
hearing aid ta akoostika
heart i karthia
heart attack i karthiaki prosvoli
heating i THermansi
heavy varis
heel to takooni
hello ya soo
help (noun) i voiTHia
  (verb) voiTHo
  help! voiTHia!

hepatitis ipatitida
her: **it's her** afti ine
  it's for her ine ya ftin
  give it to her thostis to
  her book to vivlio tis
  her house to spiti tis
  her shoes ta papootsia tis
  it's hers ine thiko tis
high psilos
highway code o othikos kothikas
hill o lofos
him: **it's him** aftos ine
  it's for him ine ya fton
  give it to him thostoo to
hire nikiazo
his: **his book** to vivlio too
  his house to spiti too
  his shoes ta papootsia too
  it's his ine thiko too
history i istoria
hitchhike kano oto-stop
HIV positive thetikos foreas 'AIDS'
hobby to 'hobby'
holiday i thiakopes
Holland i Olanthia
homeopathy omiopathitiki
homosexual o omofilofilos
honest timios
honey to meli
honeymoon o minas too melitos
horn (car) to klaxon
  (animal) to kerato
horrible fovero
hospital to nosokomio
hot water bottle i THermofora
hour i ora
house to spiti
how? pos?
hungry: I'm hungry pinao
hurry: I'm in a hurry viazome
husband o sizigos

114

I ego
ice o pagos
ice cream to pago<u>to</u>
ice cube to pagaki
ice lolly to pago<u>to</u> xilaki
if e<u>an</u>
ignition i m<u>i</u>za
ill arostos
immediately am<u>e</u>sos
impossible ath<u>i</u>nato
in m<u>e</u>sa
India i Inth<u>i</u>a
Indian (man) o Inth<u>o</u>s
  (woman) i Inth<u>i</u>
  (adj) Inth<u>i</u>kos
indicator o th<u>i</u>ktis
indigestion i thisp<u>e</u>ps<u>i</u>a
infection i m<u>o</u>linsi
information i plirofor<u>i</u>es
injection i <u>e</u>nesi
injury to at<u>i</u>hima
ink to mel<u>a</u>ni
inner tube i sabr<u>e</u>la
insect to <u>e</u>ndomo
insect repellent o apoтнi<u>tis</u> ed<u>o</u>mon
insomnia i aipn<u>i</u>a
insurance i asf<u>a</u>lia
interesting enthiaf<u>e</u>ron
internet to internet
interpret thiermin<u>e</u>vo
invitation i pr<u>o</u>sklisi
Ireland i Irlanth<u>i</u>a
Irish Irlanthik<u>o</u>s
Irishman o Irlanth<u>o</u>s
Irishwoman i Irlanth<u>e</u>za
iron (metal, for clothes) to s<u>i</u>thero
ironmonger o s<u>i</u>theras
is: he/she/it is ... <u>i</u>ne ...
island to nis<u>i</u>
it aft<u>o</u>
itch (noun) i fag<u>oo</u>ra
  it itches me tr<u>oi</u>

jacket to sak<u>a</u>ki
jacuzzi to 'jacuzzi'
jam i marmel<u>a</u>tha
jazz i 'jazz'
jealous zil<u>i</u>aris
jeans to 'jean'
jellyfish i ts<u>oo</u>htra
jeweller to kosmimatopol<u>i</u>o
job i thool<u>i</u>a
jog (verb) k<u>a</u>no 'jogging'
  to go for a jog p<u>a</u>o ya 'jogging'
joke to ast<u>i</u>o
journey to tax<u>i</u>thi
jumper to pool<u>o</u>ver
just: it's just arrived
  m<u>o</u>lis <u>e</u>ftase
  I've just one left
  <u>e</u>ho m<u>o</u>no <u>e</u>na

key to klith<u>i</u>
kidney to nefr<u>o</u>
kilo to kil<u>o</u>
kilometre to hili<u>o</u>metro
kitchen i kooz<u>i</u>na
knee to g<u>o</u>nato
knife to mah<u>e</u>ri
knit pl<u>e</u>ko
knitting needle i vel<u>o</u>na plex<u>i</u>matos
know: I don't know then x<u>e</u>ro

label i etik<u>e</u>ta
lace i thant<u>e</u>la
laces (of shoe) ta korth<u>o</u>nia
lake i l<u>i</u>mni
lamb to arn<u>i</u>
lamp i l<u>a</u>ba
lampshade to labat<u>e</u>r
land (noun) i yi
  (verb) prosyi<u>o</u>nome
language i gl<u>o</u>sa
large meg<u>a</u>los

last *(final)* telefteos
  last week i perasmeni evthomatha
  last month o perasmenos minas
  at last! epi teloos!
late: **it's getting late** vrathiazi
  the bus is late to leoforio aryise
laugh to yelio
launderette to plindirio roohon
laundry *(place)* to kaтнaristirio
  (dirty clothes) ta aplita
laxative to kaтнartiko
lazy tebelis
leaf to filo
leaflet to thiafimistiko
learn maтнeno
leather to therma
left *(not right)* aristera
  there's nothing left
  then emine tipota
left luggage o horos filaxis aposkevon
  (locker) to doolapi ton aposkevon
leftovers ta apominaria
leg to pothi
lemon to lemoni
lemonade i lemonatha
length to mikos
lens o fakos
less ligotera
lesson to maтнima
letter to grama
letter box to gramatokivotio
lettuce to marooli
library i vivlioтнiki
licence i athia
life i zoi
lift *(in building)* to ansanser
  could you give me a lift?
  borite na me pate?
light *(not heavy)* elafris
  (not dark) apalos
light meter to fotometro
lighter o anaptiras
lighter fuel to aerio anaptira

like: **I like you** moo aresis
  I like swimming moo aresi to
  kolibi
  it's like … miazi me …
lime *(fruit)* to kitro
lip salve to vootiro kakao
lipstick to krayion
liqueur to liker
list i lista
litre to litro
litter ta skoopithia
little *(small)* mikros
  it's a little big ine ligo megalo
  just a little ligaki
liver to sikoti
lobster o astakos
lollipop to glifitzoori
long makris
  how long does it take? posi ora kani?
lorry to fortigo
lost property i hamenes aposkeves
lot: **a lot** pola
loud thinatos
  (colour) htipitos
lounge to saloni
love *(noun)* i agapi
  (verb) agapo
lover *(man)* o erastis
  (woman) i eromeni
low hamilos
luck i tihi
  good luck! kali tihi!
luggage i aposkeves
luggage rack i skara
lunch to yevma

magazine to periothiko
mail ta gramata
make kano
make-up to 'make-up'
man o andras
manager o thiefтнindis

map o hartis
  a map of Athens
  enas hartis tis ATHinas
marble to marmaro
margarine i margarini
market i agora
marmalade i marmelatha
married pandremenos
mascara i maskara
mass *(church)* i litoorgia
mast to katarti
match *(light)* to spirto
  (sport) to 'match'
material *(cloth)* to ifasma
mattress to stroma
maybe isos
me: it's me ego ime
  it's for me ine ya mena
  give it to me thosto moo
meal to yevma
meat to kreas
mechanic o mihanikos
medicine to farmako
meeting i sinandisis
melon to peponi
men's *(toilet)* i tooaleta anthron
menu to menoo
message to minima
midday to mesimeri
middle: in the middle sti mesi
midnight ta mesanihta
milk to gala
mine: it's mine ine thiko moo
mineral water to emfialomeno nero
minute to lepto
mirror o kaTHreftis
mistake to laTHos
  to make a mistake kano laTHos
mobile phone o kinito tilefono
modem to modem
monastery to monastiri
money ta lefta
month o minas

monument to mnimio
moon to fegari
moped to mihanaki me petalia
more perisoteros
  more or less pano-kato
morning to proi
  in the morning to proi
mosaic to psifithoto
mosquito to koonoopi
mother i mitera
motorbike to mihanaki
motorboat varka me mihani
motorway i eTHniki othos
mountain to voono
mouse to pondiki
moustache to moostaki
mouth to stoma
move metakino
  don't move
  ! mi kooniese!
  (house) metakomizo
movie to ergo
Mr kirios
Mrs kiria
much: not much ohi poli
mug i koopa
  a mug of coffee
  ena flitzani kafe
mule to moolari
mum i mama
museum to moosio
mushroom to manitari
music i moosiki
musical instrument
  to moosiko organo
musician o moosikos
mussels ta mithia
mustard i moostartha
my: my book to vivlio moo
  my bag i tsanda moo
  my keys ta klithia moo
mythology i miTHoloyia

nail *(metal)* to karfi
  (finger) to nihi
nailfile i lima nihion
nail polish to mano
name to onoma
nappy i pana
narrow stenos
near: near the door konda sti porta
  near London konda sto Lonthino
necessary aparetitos
necklace to kolie
need *(verb)* hriazome
  I need ... hriazome ...
  there's no need then hriazete
needle i velona
negative *(photo)* to arnitiko
neither: neither of them kanenas
  apo aftoos
  neither ... nor ...
  oote ... oote ...
nephew o anipsios
never pote
new kenooryios
news ta nea
newsagent to praktorio
  efimerithon
newspaper i efimeritha
New Zealand i Nea Zilanthia
New Zealander
  (man) o Neozilanthos
  (woman) i Neozilantheza
next epomenos
  next week i epomeni
  evthomatha
  next month o epomenos minas
  what next? ti alo?
nice oreos
niece i anipsia
night i nihta
nightclub to nihterino kendro
nightdress to nihtiko
no *(response)* ohi
  I have no money then eho lefta

noisy THorivothis
north o voras
Northern Ireland i Voria Irlanthia
nose i miti
not then
notebook to blokaki
nothing tipota
novel to miTHistorima
now tora
nowhere pooTHena
nudist o yimnistis
number o ariTHmos
number plate i pinakitha
nurse i nosokoma
nut *(fruit)* i xiri karpi
  (for bolt) to paximathi

occasionally pote-pote
octopus to htapothi
of too
office to grafio
often sihna
oil to lathi
ointment i alifi
OK endaxi
old palios
olive i elia
omelette i omeleta
on pano
one enas, mia, ena
onion to kremithi
only mono
open *(verb)* anigo
  (adj) anihtos
opposite: opposite the hotel
  apenandi apo to xenothohio
optician o optikos
or i
orange *(colour)* portokali
  (fruit) to portokali
orange juice i portokalatha
orchestra i orhistra

ordinary *(normal)* kanonikos
organ to organo
  (music) to armonio
our thikos mas
  it's ours ine thiko mas
out: he's out ine exo
outside exo
over pano apo
  over there eki pera
overtake prosperno
oyster to strithi

pack of cards i trapoola
package to paketo
  (parcel) to thema
packet to paketo
  a packet of … ena paketo …
padlock to looketo
page i selitha
pain o ponos
paint *(noun)* to hroma
pair to zevgari
Pakistan to Pakistan
Pakistani *(man)* o Pakistanos
  (woman) i Pakistani
  (adj) Pakistanikos
pale hlomos
pancakes i thiples
paper to harti
paracetamol to pafsipono
parcel to thema
pardon? signomi?
parents i gonis
park *(noun)* to parko
  (verb) parkaro
parsley o maindanos
party *(celebration)* to parti
  (group) to groop
  (political) to koma
passenger epivatis
passport to thiavatirio
pasta ta zimarika

path to monopati
pavement to pezothromio
pay plirono
peach to rothakino
peanuts ta fistikia
pear to ahlathi
pearl to margaritari
peas ta bizelia
pedestrian o pezos
peg *(clothes)* i kremastra
pen to stilo
pencil to molivi
pencil sharpener i xistra
penfriend o filos thi' alilografias
peninsula i hersonisos
penknife o sooyas
people i anthropi
pepper *(& salt)* to piperi
  (red/green) i piperia
peppermints i mendes
per: per night tin vrathia
perfect telios
perfume to aroma
perhaps isos
perm i permanant
petrol i venzini
petrol station to venzinathiko
personal stereo to 'Walkman'®
petticoat to kombinezon
photocopier to fototipiko mihanima
photograph *(noun)* i fotografia
  (verb) fotografizo
photographer o fotografos
phrase book to vivlio xenon thialogon
piano to piano
pickpocket o portofolas
picnic to 'picnic'
pillow to maxilari
pilot o pilotos
pin i karfitsa
pine *(tree)* to pefko
pineapple o ananas
pink roz

pipe (*for smoking*) to tsib<u>oo</u>ki
  (*for water*) i sol<u>i</u>na
piston to pist<u>o</u>ni
pizza i p<u>i</u>zza
place to m<u>e</u>ros
plant to f<u>i</u>to
plaster (*for cut*) o lefkopl<u>a</u>stis
plastic to plastik<u>o</u>
plastic bag i plastik<u>i</u> sak<u>oo</u>la
plate to pi<u>a</u>to
platform i platf<u>o</u>rma
play (*theatre*) to тнeatrik<u>o</u> <u>e</u>rgo
please parakal<u>o</u>
plug (*electrical*) i br<u>i</u>sa
  (*sink*) to v<u>oo</u>loma
pocket i ts<u>e</u>pi
poison to thilit<u>i</u>rio
police i astinom<u>i</u>a
police officer o astinomik<u>o</u>s
police station
  to astinomik<u>o</u> tm<u>i</u>ma
politics ta politik<u>a</u>
poor ftoh<u>o</u>s
  (*bad quality*) kak<u>o</u>s
pop music i pop moosik<u>i</u>
pork to hir<u>i</u>no
port (*harbour*) to lim<u>a</u>ni
porter (*for luggage*) o ah-тнof<u>o</u>ros
  (*hotel*) o тнiror<u>o</u>s
possible thinat<u>o</u>n
post (*noun*) ta gr<u>a</u>mata
  (*verb*) tahithrom<u>o</u>
postbox to gramatokiv<u>o</u>tio
postcard i kart-post<u>a</u>l
poster to p<u>o</u>ster
post office to tahithrom<u>i</u>o
postman o tahithr<u>o</u>mos
potato i pat<u>a</u>ta
poultry ta pooler<u>i</u>ka
pound (*money*) i l<u>i</u>ra
  (*weight*) i l<u>i</u>bra
powder i sk<u>o</u>ni
pram to karots<u>a</u>ki

prawn i gar<u>i</u>tha
  (*bigger*) i karav<u>i</u>tha
prescription i sind<u>a</u>yi
pretty (*beautiful*) <u>o</u>morfos
  (*quite*) arket<u>a</u>
priest o pap<u>a</u>s
private ithiotik<u>o</u>s
problem to pr<u>o</u>vlima
  what's the problem?
  ti simv<u>e</u>ni
public to kin<u>o</u>
pull trav<u>o</u>
puncture to k<u>e</u>ndima
purple porfir<u>o</u>
purse to portof<u>o</u>li
push spr<u>o</u>hno
pushchair to karots<u>a</u>ki
pyjamas i pitz<u>a</u>mes

quality i pi<u>o</u>tita
quay i prokim<u>e</u>a
question i er<u>o</u>tisi
queue (*noun*) i o<u>o</u>ra
  (*verb*) b<u>e</u>no stin o<u>o</u>ra
quick grigoros
quiet is<u>i</u>hos
quite (*fairly*) arket<u>a</u>
  (*fully*) tel<u>i</u>os

radiator to psiy<u>i</u>o
radio to rathi<u>o</u>fono
radish to rapan<u>a</u>ki
railway line i gram<u>e</u>s too tr<u>e</u>noo
rain i vroh<u>i</u>
raincoat to athi<u>a</u>vroho
raisins i staf<u>i</u>thes
rare (*uncommon*) sp<u>a</u>nios
  (*steak*) misopsim<u>e</u>nos
rat o aroor<u>e</u>gos
razor blades ta xiraf<u>a</u>kia
read thiav<u>a</u>zo

120

reading lamp to fos too grafioo
  (bed) to potatif
ready etimos
rear lights ta piso fota
receipt i apothixi
receptionist o reseptionistas
record *(music)* o thiskos
  (sporting etc) to rekor
record player to pik-ap
record shop to thiskopolio
red kokino
refreshments ta anapsiktika
registered letter to sistimeno
  grama
relative o sigenis
relax iremo
religion i THriskia
remember THimame
  I don't remember then THimame
rent *(verb)* nikiazo
reservation to klisimo THesis
rest *(remainder)* to ipolipo
  (relax) xekoorazome
restaurant to estiatorio
restaurant car to estiatorio trenoo
return epistrefo
Rhodes i Rothos
rice to rizi
rich ploosios
right *(correct)* sostos
  (direction) thexia
ring *(to call)* tilefono
  (wedding etc) to thahtilithi
ripe orimos
river to potami
road o thromos
rock *(stone)* o vrahos
  (music) i moosiki rok
roll *(bread)* to psomaki
  (verb) kilo
roller skates ta patinia
roof i orofi
  (flat) i taratsa

room to thomatio
  (space) to meros
rope to s-hini
rose to triandafilo
round *(circular)* strogilos
  it's my round ine i sira moo
rowing boat i varka me koopia
rubber *(eraser)* i goma
  (material) to lastiho
rubbish ta skoopithia
ruby *(stone)* to roobini
rucksack to sakithio
rug *(mat)* to halaki
  (blanket) i kooverta
ruins ta eripia
ruler o harakas
rum to roomi
run *(person)* treho
runway o thiathromos

sad lipimenos
safe asfalis
safety pin i paramana
sailing boat to istioforo
salad i salata
salami to salami
sale *(at reduced prices)* i ekptosis
salmon o solomos
salt to alati
same: the same dress
  to ithio forema
  the same people i ithi-i anthropi
  same again, please ena akoma
sand i amos
sandals ta sandalia
sand dunes i amolofi
sandwich to 'sandwich'
sanitary towels i servietes
satellite TV i thoriforiki tileorasi
sauce i saltsa
saucepan i katsarola
sauna i sa-oona

sausage to lookaniko
say lego
  what did you say? ti ipes?
  how do you say ...? pos THa poome ...?
scarf to kaskol
  (head) to mandili
school to s-holio
scissors to psalithi
Scotland i Skotia
Scottish Skotsezikos
screw i vitha
screwdriver to katsavithi
sea i THalasa
seafood ta THalasina
seat i THesi
seat belt i zoni asfalias
second thefteros
see kitazo
  I can't see then vlepo
  I see katalava
sell poolo
separate xehoristos
separated horismenos
Sellotape® to 'sellotape'
serious sovaros
serviette i hartopetseta
several arketi
sew ravo
shampoo to sambooan
shave *(noun)* to xirisma
  (verb) xirizome
shaving foam o afros xirismatos
shawl to sali
she afti
sheet to sendoni
shell to ostrako
sherry to seri
ship to karavi
shirt to pookamiso
shoelaces ta korthonia
shoe polish to verniki papootsion
shoes ta papootsia

shoe shop to katastima ipothimaton
shop to magazi
shopping ta psonia
  to go shopping pao ya psonia
short kondos
shorts to 'shorts'
shoulder o omos
shower *(bath)* to doos
  (rain) i bora
shower gel to zele ya doos
shrimp i garitha
shutter *(camera)* to thiafragma
  (window) i pantzoori
sick *(ill)* arostos
  I feel sick ime athiaTHetos
side *(edge)* plevra
  I'm on her side ime me to meros tis
sidelights ta fota porias
sights: the sights of ... ta axioTHeata tis ...
silk to metaxoto
silver *(colour)* asimi
  (metal) to asimi
simple aplos
sing tragootho
single *(one)* monos
  (unmarried) anipandros
single room to mono thomatio
sister i athelfi
skid *(verb)* glistrao
skin cleanser to galaktoma kaTHarismoo
skirt i foosta
sky o oooranos
sleep *(noun)* o ipnos
  (verb) kimame
  to go to sleep pao ya ipno
sleeping bag to 'sleeping bag'
sleeping pill to ipnotiko hapi
slippers i pandofles
slow argos
small mikros

smell *(noun)* i mirothi̱a
  (verb) miri̱zo
smile *(noun)* to hamo̱yelo
  (verb) hamoyeḻo
smoke *(noun)* o kapno̱s
  (verb) kapni̱zo
snack to pro̱hiro yevma
snorkel o anapnefsti̱ras
snow to hi̱oni
so: so good poli̱ kala̱
  not so much o̱hi to̱so poli̱
soaking solution *(for contact lenses)*
  igro̱ sindi̱risis fako̱n epafi̱s
socks i ka̱ltses
soda water i so̱tha
soft lenses i malaki̱ faki̱ epafi̱s
somebody ka̱pios
somehow ka̱pos
something ka̱ti
sometimes meriko̱s fore̱s
somewhere kapo̱o
son o yio̱s
song to trago̱othi
sorry! pardo̱n!
  I'm sorry sigṉomi
soup i so̱opa
south o no̱tos
South Africa i No̱tios Afriki̱
South African
  (man) o Notioafrika̱nos
  (woman) i Notioafrika̱na
  (adj) Notioafrika̱nikos
souvenir to enTHi̱mio
spade *(shovel)* to ftia̱ri
  (cards) to basto̱oni
Spain i Ispani̱a
Spanish *(adj)* Ispaniko̱s
spanner to klithi̱
spares ta andalaktika̱
spark(ing) plug to boozi̱
speak mila̱o
  do you speak ...? mila̱te ...?
  I don't speak ... then milo̱ ...

speed i tahi̱tita
speed limit to o̱rio tahi̱titos
speedometer to konte̱r
spider i ara̱hni
spinach to spana̱ki
spoon to koota̱li
sprain to strabo̱oligma
spring *(mechanical)* to elati̱rio
  (season) i a̱nixi
stadium to sta̱thio
staircase i ska̱la
stairs ta skalopa̱tia
stamp to gramato̱simo
stapler o sintheti̱ras
star to aste̱ri
  (film) i star
start i arhi̱
  (verb) arhi̱zo
station o staTHmo̱s
statue to a̱galma
steak i brizo̱la
steal kle̱vo
  it's been stolen to klepsa̱ne
steering wheel to timo̱ni
stewardess i aerosinotho̱s
sting *(noun)* to tso̱oximo
  (verb) tso̱ozo
  it stings tso̱ozi
stockings i ka̱ltses
stomach to stoma̱hi
stomachache o stomaho̱ponos
stop *(verb)* stamato̱
  (bus stop) i sta̱si
  stop! stama̱ta!
storm i THi̱ela
strawberry i fra̱oola
stream *(small river)* to potama̱ki
street o thro̱mos
string *(cord)* o spa̱gos
  (guitar etc) i horthi̱
student o maTHiti̱s
stupid vla̱kas
suburbs ta proa̱stia

sugar i zahari
suit (*noun*) to koostoomi
    (*verb*) teriazo
    it suits you soo pai
suitcase i valitsa
sun o ilios
sunbathe kano ilioTHerapia
sunburn to kapsimo apo ton ilio
sunglasses ta yalia ilioo
sunny: it's sunny ehi liakatha
suntan to mavrisma
suntan lotion to andiliako
supermarket to 'supermarket'
supplement epipleon
surname to epiTHeto
sweat (*noun*) o ithrotas
    (*verb*) ithrono
sweatshirt i fanela
sweet (*not sour*) glikos
    (*candy*) i karamela
swimming costume to mayio
swimming pool i pisina
swimming trunks to mayio
Swiss (*man*) o Elvetos
    (*woman*) i Elvetitha
    (*adj*) Elvetikos
switch o thiakoptis
Switzerland i Elvetia
synagogue i sinagoyi

table to trapezi
tablet to thiskio
take perno
take-away ya to thromo
takeoff (*noun*) i apoyiosi
take off (*verb*) apoyionome
talcum powder to talk
talk (*noun*) i sizitisi
    (*verb*) milo
tall psilos
tampon to 'Tampax'®
tangerine to mandarini

tap i vrisi
tapestry i tapetsaria
tea to tsai
tea towel i petseta
telegram to tilegrafima
telephone (*noun*) to tilefono
    (*verb*) tilefono
telephone box o tilefonikos THalamos
telephone call to tilefonima
television i tfleorasi
temperature i THermokrasia
tent i skini
tent peg o pasalos skinis
tent pole o stilos skinis
thank (*verb*) efharisto
    thanks efharisto
    thank you sas efharisto
that: that bus ekino to leoforio
    that man ekinos o andras
    that woman ekini i yineka
    what's that? ti ine ekino?
    I think that … nomizo oti …
their: their room to thomatio toos
    their books ta vivlia toos
    it's theirs ine thiko toos
them: it's them afti ine
    it's for them ine yaftoos
    give it to them thosto toos
then tote
there eki
thermos flask o THermos
these: these things
    afta ta pragmata
    these are mine
    afta ine thika moo
they afti
thick pahis
thin leptos
think nomizo/skeftome
    I think so etsi nomizo
    I'll think about it
    THa to skefto
thirsty: I'm thirsty thipso

this: this bus afto to leoforio
  this man aftos o andras
  this woman afti i yineka
  what's this? ti ine afto?
  this is Mr ... apotho o kirios ...
those: those things afta ta pragmata
  those are his afta ine thika too
throat o lemos
throat pastilles i pastilles lemoo
thunderstorm i kateyitha
ticket to isitirio
tie (noun) i gravata
  (verb) theno
time i ora
  what's the time? ti ora ine?
timetable to programa
tin i konserva
tin opener to anihtiri
tip (money) to poorbooar
  (end) miti
tired koorasmenos
  I feel tired ime koorasmenos
tissues ta hartomandila
to: to England stin Anglia
  to the station sto staTHmo
  to the doctor sto yatro
toast to tost
tobacco o kapnos
toilet i tooaleta
toilet paper to harti iyias
tomato i domata
tomorrow avrio
tongue i glosa
tonic to 'tonic'
tonight apopse
too (also) episis
  (excessive) para poli
toothache o ponothondos
toothbrush i othondovoortsa
toothpaste i othondokrema
torch o fakos
tour i peri-iyisi
tourist o tooristas

towel i petseta
tower o pirgos
town i poli
town hall to thimarhio
toy to pehnithi
toy shop to katastima pehnithion
track suit i aTHlitiki forma
tractor to trakter
tradition i parathosi
traffic i kinisi
traffic lights ta fanaria
trailer to rimoolko
train to treno
translate metafrazo
transmission (for car) i metathosi
  kiniseos
travel agency to taxithiotiko
  grafio
traveller's cheque i taxithiotiki
  epitayi
tray o thiskos
tree to thendro
trousers to pandeloni
try prospaTHo
tunnel i siraga
Turk (man) o Toorkos
  (woman) i Toorkala
Turkey i Toorkia
Turkish Toorkikos
tweezers ta tsibithaki
typewriter i grafomihani
tyre to lastiho

umbrella i obrela
uncle o THios
under kato
underground o ipoyios
underpants to sovrako
university to panepistimio
unmarried anipandros
until mehri
unusual asiniTHistos

up pano
  (upwards) pros ta pano
urgent epigon
us: it's us emis imaste
  it's for us ine ya mas
  give it to us thosto mas
use *(noun)* i hrisimotis
  (verb) hrisimopio
  it's no use
then axizi ton kopo
useful hrisimos
usual siniTHismenos
usually siniTHos

vacancy *(room)* kenos
vacuum cleaner i ilektriki skoopa
vacuum flask o THermos
valley i kilatha
valve i valvitha
vanilla i vanilia
vase to vazo
veal to mos-haraki
vegetables ta lahanika
vegetarian *(person)* o hortofagos
vehicle to trohoforo
very poli
vest to fanelaki
view i THea
viewfinder to skopeftro
villa i 'villa'
village to horio
vinegar to xithi
violin to violi
visa i viza
visit *(noun)* i episkepsi
  (verb) episkeptome
visitor o episkeptis
vitamin tablet i vitamini
vodka i vodka
voice i foni

waiter o servitoros
  waiter! garson!
waiting room to saloni
waitress i garsona
Wales i Ooalia
walk *(noun)* to perpatima
  (verb) perpato
  to go for a walk pao volta
wall o tihos
wallet to portofoli
war o polemos
wardrobe i doolapa
warm zestos
was: I was imoon
  he was itan
  she was itan
  it was itan
washing powder to aporipandiko
washing-up liquid to sapooni piaton
wasp i sfiga
watch *(noun)* to roloi
  (verb) parakolooTHo
water to nero
waterfall o katarahtis
wave *(noun)* to kima
  (verb) hereto
we emis
weather o keros
Web site to web site
wedding o gamos
week i evthomatha
wellingtons i galotses
Welsh Ooalikos
were: we were imastan
  you were isastan
  (sing. familiar) isoon
  they were itan
west thitikos
wet vregmenos
what? ti?
wheel i rotha
wheelchair i anapiriki polithrona
when? pote?

where? poo?
whether kata poso
which? pios?
whisky to 'whisky'
white aspros
who? pios?
why? yati?
wide platis
wife i sizigos
wind o anemos
window to paraTHiro
windscreen to parbriz
windscreen wiper o ialokaTHaristiras
wine to krasi
wine list o katalogos krasion
wing to ftero
with me
without horis
women (toilet) i tooaleta yinekon
wood to xilo
wool to mali
word i lexi
work (noun) i thoolia
   (verb) thoolevo
wrapping paper harti peritiligmatos
   (for presents) harti ya thora
wrist o karpos

writing paper to harti alilografias
wrong laTHos

year o hronos
yellow kitrinos
yes ne
yesterday htes
yet akoma
   not yet ohi akoma
yoghurt to yaoorti
you esis
   (sing. familiar) esi
your: your book
   (familiar) to vivlio soo
   (polite) to vivlio sas
   your shoes
   (familiar) ta papootsia soo
   (polite) ta papootsia sas
yours: is it yours?
   (familiar) ine thiko soo?
   (polite) ine thiko sas?
youth hostel o xenonas neon

zip to fermooar
zoo o zo-oloyikos kipos

127